DEVELOPMENTAL MOVEMENT FOR CHILDREN

Mainstream, special needs and pre-school

VERONICA SHERBORNE

Former Senior Lecturer in Special Education,
Bristol Polytechnic
Clive Landen, Chief Photographer

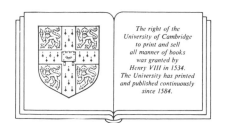

The right of the
University of Cambridge
to print and sell
all manner of books
was granted by
Henry VIII in 1534.
The University has printed
and published continuously
since 1584.

Cambridge University Press

Cambridge
New York   Port Chester   Melbourne   Sydney

For James

Published by the Press Syndicate of the University of Cambridge
The Pitt Building, Trumpington Street, Cambridge CB2 1RP
40 West 20th Street, New York, NY 10011, USA
10 Stamford Road, Oakleigh, Melbourne 3166, Australia

First published 1990

Printed in Great Britain by Scotprint Ltd

British Library cataloguing in publication data applied for

ISBN 0 521 37006 X hard covers
ISBN 0 521 37903 2 paperback

DS

Author's acknowledgements

I am indebted to the following for their help in providing the photographs which are used to illustrate this book: Swedish Press for Figs 15 and 20; Cedric Barker for Figs 11, 16 and 23; Ian Parry for Figs 32, 38 to 41 and page 53; the house parent who took the photographs in Figs 17, 18, 27, and page 89; and Clive Landen, Senior Lecturer, Documentary Photography Course, Newport College of Higher Education, Gwent, for all the other photographs.

The photographs are of children from the following schools:

Grimsbury Park School, Bristol
St Paul's Day Nursery, Bristol
Elmfield School for the Deaf, Bristol
Westhaven School, Weston-super-Mare
Warley Manor, Bath
Romney Avenue Infant and Junior Schools, Bristol
Henbury Court Junior School, Hearing Impaired Unit, Bristol
Ravenswood School, Nailsea, Bristol
Highwood School, Bristol
Stoke Leys School, Aylesbury
Cedars Middle School, Harrow
Whittlesea School, Harrow

The handwriting extracts in Appendix 2 were rewritten by first-year pupils at Comberton Village College, Cambridgeshire.
Text design by Heather Richards

Contents

Introduction

This book is for teachers in many fields, for parents, student teachers, social workers, educational psychologists, and indeed for everyone concerned with the development of children.

The book is divided into four main sections: Part One, What to teach (Chapters 1 and 2), Part Two, Why we teach it (Chapters 3 and 4), Part Three, How to teach it (Chapter 5), and Part Four, which describes the needs of children and adults who present special challenges (Chapters 6 and 7). The final section, Part Five, is a brief summary of the theory of developmental movement. Chapter 1 will be particularly useful to social workers and nurses, and together the first two chapters will be especially helpful to teachers and physiotherapists.

The theory underlying *Developmental movement for children* which I have developed is based on Rudolf Laban's analysis of human movement. There are many of us who owe a great debt to Laban and his work. In Germany, before the last war, he applied his theories to dance and dance production, and to movement choirs involving hundreds of people. In Britain he applied his theories to work in industry, to the movement training of actors and – through his colleague Lisa Ullmann – to the movement and dance of children. In all the wide-ranging application of his theories, Laban's aim was not so much to make successful performers as to develop the personality, to develop potential, and to help people to understand and experience the widest range of movement possible.

I trained initially in physical education and physiotherapy, but later was fortunate enough to be taught by Laban, and by Ullmann, at the Art of Movement Studio in Manchester. It was a difficult transition to make from the gymnastics of my first training, but from Laban I learnt a different understanding and awareness of the human body and its movement.

In my own work I have applied Laban's theories to the needs of mainstream children, children with special needs, and pre-school children. During the last thirty years I have worked with classroom teachers, physical education teachers, drama teachers, physiotherapists, speech therapists, occupational therapists, nurses, nursery teachers, nursery nurses and teachers in special education, and I have brought up three children of my own. Through my experience of teaching and observing human movement, and of learning through trial and error, I have come to the conclusion that all children have two basic needs: they need to feel at home in their own bodies and so to gain body mastery, and they need to be able to form relationships. The fulfilment of these needs – relating to oneself and to other people – can be achieved through good movement teaching.

When I began to train students to teach children with severe learning difficulties, my first aim was to help the students to work together and to feel secure within the group using partner and group activities. To my surprise the students went on to introduce some of the partner activities to the children with severe learning difficulties, with some success, and it became clear to me that the children too could relate to each other in the kind of activities that are described in Chapter 1. I later found that this approach to movement teaching was equally relevant to mainstream children. This was also a new idea to me, and an important discovery.

The activities described in this book are referred to here as 'experiences' rather than 'exercises' because they combine both physical and psychological learning experiences. Underlying all these activities are certain beliefs:

- Movement experiences are fundamental to the development of all children but are particularly important to children with special needs who often have difficulty in relating to their own bodies and to other people.
- The input or 'feeding in' of movement experiences has to be more concentrated and more continuous for children with special needs than for children in mainstream schools.

Many parents and caregivers, when they play physically with children, instinctively use many of the activities I have described in Chapter 1. In this book I have analysed and categorised a variety of these activities and have adapted relationship play to the needs of all children. A number of the experiences described in this book are illustrated in the films and videos which are listed on page 121.

It is essential to help all children to concentrate on the experiences described so that they become aware of what is happening in their bodies. In this way they are able to learn from their movement experiences. I call this 'listening' to the body.

Children described in this book as children with special needs are children with severe learning difficulties, children with moderate learning difficulties, children with profound and multiple learning difficulties, children who are emotionally and behaviourally disturbed, and children who are hearing impaired.

Several analyses of my work have been made in recent years, including a dissertation for an MA degree in the Department of Physical Education at the University of Leeds, and a dissertation for a B Ed in Special Education for the Council for National Academic Awards; the Carnegie UK Trust has also awarded a grant for research into my work. Now the time has come for me to write about my work myself.

Veronica Sherborne

Part One | *WHAT TO TEACH*

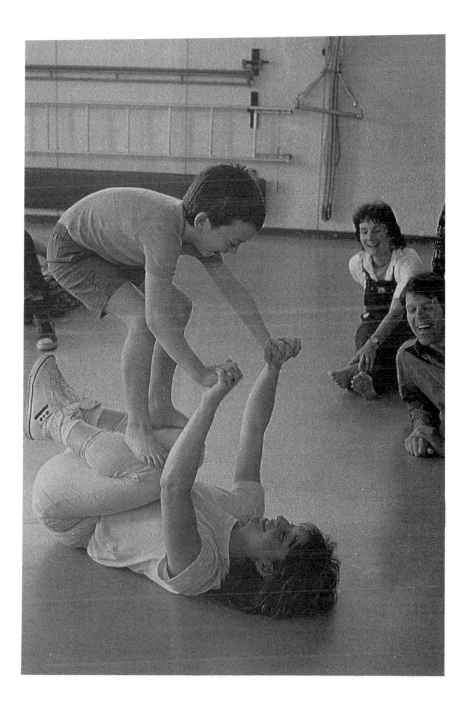

1

Developing relationships

It is impossible to say which comes first, self-awareness or awareness of others. Because it is easier to explain and illustrate, awareness of others is dealt with first here.

Relationship play requires a one-to-one relationship in which a more able, more mature person partners a younger, less able partner, usually a child. Both partners gain from the experience, as they have much to give each other.

There are many ways of organising partners. Parent and child is the ideal partnership, but is not always possible. Student teachers benefit from relationship play with mainstream children as well as with those with special needs, and young people in secondary schools can make supportive partners for children with special needs. Nursery nurses can partner pre-school children. Partners can be found within a school, or be from another local institution. Children in a mainstream class can partner each other, or older children with mild learning difficulties can partner younger children with severe learning difficulties. Primary school children can partner younger children in their school or can work with children with special needs. Senior children with severe learning difficulties, with careful help and preparation, can partner each other, or can learn to partner children with profound and multiple learning difficulties. There are a number of photographs on the following pages which illustrate well the variety of possible partnerships.

The aims of relationship play

Self-confidence

The younger child gains confidence from the way he or she is physically supported; the child finds it safe to commit and trust him- or herself to the care of the older partner. The quality of the interaction between the care-giver and the child has a profound effect on the child. A great deal is communicated through the quality of feeling which the older partner shows to the younger partner. The young child should experience suc-

Note The activities described in Chapters 1 and 2 are summarised in Appendix 1, pages 112–15.

cess, a sense a achievement, and an awareness of self-worth. The younger child should become confident enough to show initiative in the way he or she responds to the older partner.

Body knowledge

The child develops body awareness as he or she experiences the body against that of the older partner. The younger child experiences the trunk, the centre of the body and the link between the extremities, in many of the relationship-play activities described here. This helps the child to develop a sense of wholeness, and an awareness that the parts of the body are well connected to each other. The development of body awareness is described in Chapter 2.

Physical and emotional security

When the less able child finds he or she can trust a partner to physically support, contain and handle him or her in a trustworthy way, that child develops not only physical confidence but also a sense of being emotionally secure. Relationship play can be especially beneficial for children who are emotionally and socially insecure.

Communication

One of the advantages of relationship play is the development of a variety of ways of communicating. Initially the young child may have no language and may passively receive movement experiences. Later the child may respond so that a dialogue of shared movement play develops. The child may then take the initiative and reverse roles with the partner, and may start to introduce new ideas into the play situation. The child may have little or no language but can communicate quite clearly through movement play. The caregiver has to be sensitive to the signals that the child may give (see Chapter 4, Observation of movement).

The adult can help the child develop a rich vocabulary of language by encouraging a wide variety of movement activities. Words which describe actions and which are experienced in movement activities are more likely to be remembered and used than words which are not accompanied by physical experience. Such words and phrases might be 'push', 'climb', 'lie down', 'shut your eyes', 'make a house', 'strong', 'gentle'. Prepositions such as 'over', 'under', 'behind', etc. are also learnt as a result of physical experience.

An important aspect of communication is eye contact, and some activities are especially useful because they encourage this. Eye contact is necessary if the child is to concentrate and learn new skills from the caregiver.

Types of relationship play

There are three broad types of relationship:
1 Caring or 'with' relationships
2 Shared relationships
3 'Against' relationships

Caring or 'with' relationships

This type of relationship can be experienced through many different activities, several of which are described in detail here. It is best to demonstrate all activities first so that both partners know what is going to happen. As the activities become familiar this will not be necessary.

Containing a partner   On the whole it is best to start a movement session with a caring relationship in which the older partner gives a sense of security to the younger partner. The simplest form of this is for the older partner to make a 'house' or 'container' for the younger partner.

Cradling   The participants sit on the floor, with the younger partner between the legs of the older partner. The older partner enfolds the younger with the arms, legs and trunk. The older partner rocks gently from side to side, cradling the younger partner, using knees, thighs and arms to give support (Figs. 1 and 2).

The child needs to tip slightly off-balance so that the adult or older partner can feel if the child is ready to give part of his or her weight to the adult to support. When the child is able to commit some of his or her weight to the adult, this indicates that the child trusts the adult. Relaxation is helped if the older partner hums or sings quietly to accompany the cradling action. The free flow of the movement from side to side has a calming, harmonious effect. A free-flow movement is one that cannot easily be stopped once momentum has started. Controlled flow movement is described at a later stage (see page 57).

The older partner has to decide on the right tempo of the cradling and the appropriate range of the sway of the movement to suit the child. Much is communicated during this activity; giving confidence and security through cradling is a skill which the older partner learns with practice. Not all adults can contain in a secure way, possibly because they have not experienced it themselves. The ability to contain, support and use free-flow cradling varies from one caregiver to another. Some people manipulate their partners, but others are both physically adept and have good feeling, and thus give a sense of security to their partners.

Containing with free-flow rocking makes a calm ending to a movement session. The quality of containing and the degree of sensitivity involved are a good contrast to the vigorous and strong activities that have occurred during the session. The activity is also enhanced by the rapport that has been built up between the partners during the session.

When partners are of equal size, the 'container' partner can put his or her ear against the partner's back; this will help him or her to 'listen' to the

5

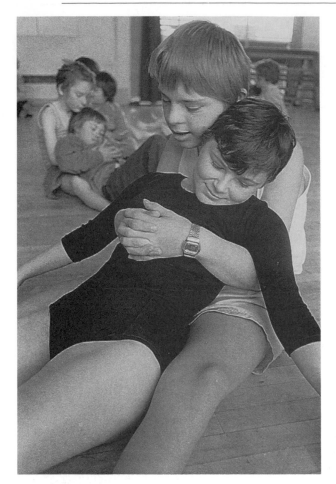

One child cradles
another in a school
for children with
severe learning
difficulties

Day nursery. Cradling
at the end of a
2 movement session

3 The author supports and cradles a profoundly deaf boy

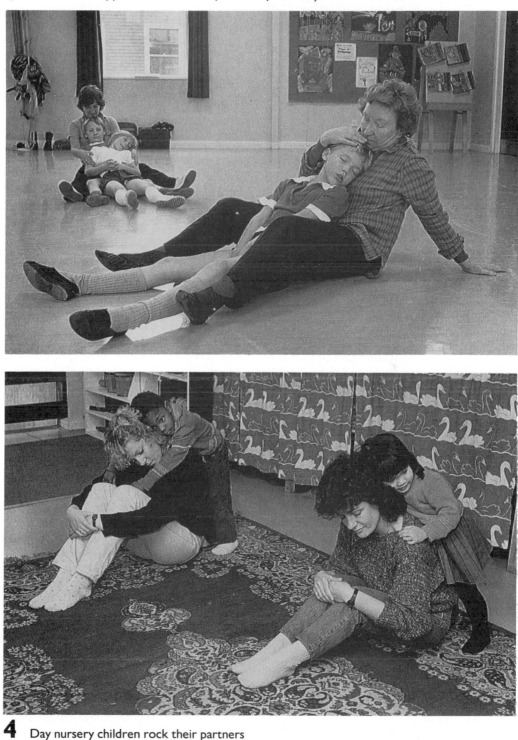

4 Day nursery children rock their partners

partner. The person who is contained may find it more comfortable, and therefore easier to relax, if he or she leans back with the head resting on the supporting partner's shoulder with legs stretched out, rather than being in a curled-up position. The supporting partner may have to put a hand on the floor behind to take the weight of the partner. Cradling is then instigated by the sway of the trunk and shoulders (Fig. 3).

For those children who dare not shut their eyes while being cradled, the supporters may use one hand lightly to cover the children's eyes. The children will then find it easier to 'listen' to and concentrate on what is going on inside their own bodies. Some children need to be contained very lightly while others enjoy the older partner completely engulfing them. Children with severe learning difficulties and young mainstream children can cradle each other sensitively and successfully. Very young children can stand behind adult partners and rock them from side to side (Fig. 4).

Rocking horses Cradling from side to side can be changed to rocking backwards and for-wards. The caregiver sits with the child between the legs, both partners facing forward, and grasps the child under the knees. Very small children can sit on the adult's thighs. The caregiver then tips back a little way, and then forwards. As the child finds it safe to be tipped back the caregiver rocks a little further back. In this activity the caregiver gives total support. Eventually the child tips so far back that he or she is upside down with feet in the air above the head. The caregiver's legs are also up in the air and both partners have an unfamiliar view of their feet above them. Children love being upside down. This activity should be accompanied by appro-priate vocal sounds, for example 'whee' or 'whoosh'. Children who are shy often relax and laugh as they play at being 'rocking horses'.

Backward somersault When children are confident, the rocking horse movement can be increased backwards so far that the child, who is upside down, continues the movement backwards over the caregiver's head and does a backward somersault, landing on knees or feet behind the caregiver's head (Figs. 5a, 5b). This activity takes courage and confidence but comes easily to agile children. The children learn to trust their partners and themselves, develop mastery of their bodies, and cope with being disoriented by being upside down and unable to see what is going on. When children cannot see, they have to trust their own body mastery and listen to what is going on in their own bodies.

Some young children, for example some socially deprived children, are not used to physical play with others, and may be reserved and lacking in self-confidence. It is helpful to create an atmosphere of play and fun. One way of achieving this is to cradle the child from side to side until the sway to one side becomes so great that both caregiver and child fall over. Children find that falling over safely in this way is fun, and usually want to repeat the experience. Sometimes pre-school children will instigate the cradling; while sitting in their 'house' or 'container' they will press on their partner's knees to make them start to sway from side to side.

These activities of falling safely and rocking backwards with legs in the air produce much laughter, even in children who find it difficult to play.

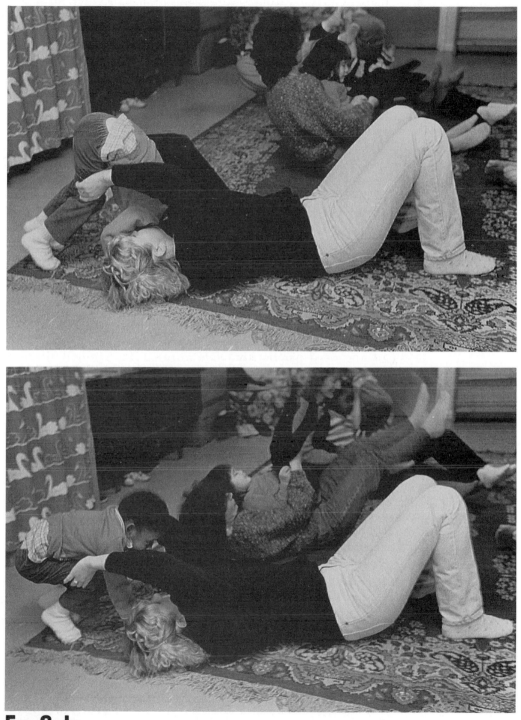

5a & b Day nursery. The end of a backward somersault

Supporting   Support can be total – that is, the whole weight is carried – or it may be partial, as for instance when a child leans against a caregiver. The following activity is undemanding and encourages a child to relate.

The adult lies down on his or her back, knees bent up, and the child sits astride the stomach so that the partners face one another. The adult can gently bounce the child up and down. The child can lean backwards on the adult's thighs and then tip forward. From this position of being higher than the adult, the child is likely to look down and make eye contact. Commitment of weight to the support of the adult indicates that the child both trusts the adult and trusts him- or herself.

The adult can lie face down and support the child astride the back. In this position the child can cling on with the legs and the adult can hump the child up and down. If the adult feels the child's legs gripping the sides of the adult's body, and perhaps the arms gripping his or her neck, this is a clear sign that the child wants to be involved with the adult. On a slippery floor the adult can creep like a lizard, carrying the child on the back. Some children who feel threatened by eye contact will accept an adult's back as a place to sit and in this way feel it is safe to commit themselves to the support of an adult. Some children initially will only accept physical contact if they are the dominant partners – that is, higher than their partners.

When working with profoundly and multiply handicapped children or adults, the caregiver lies face up and supports the handicapped person along the length of the body (Fig. 6). The caregiver can hold and rock the handicapped person from side to side. The free-flow rocking and the comfort and warmth of the caregiver's body help to reduce spasticity and often the best relaxation is achieved in this way. Eye contact may also be achieved with people who usually avoid it. Sometimes the handicapped person relaxes better on the supporter's back. The human body induces better relaxation than does a mattress or the floor.

Rolling   The experience of rolling has much to commend it. It provides an enjoyable way of 'feeding in' to the child the fact that he has a trunk; he or she feels it against the floor, mat, or other supporting surface. The child also experiences the free flow of weight and the movement of the body as a whole, which brings about a harmonious sensation. Rolling is a series of falls, the safest the body can do. It involves letting go of weight and giving in to the pull of gravity. Tense, anxious children roll rigidly like a log, with their forearms protecting the chest and the head lifted. They need help to let the body fall and give in to the pull of gravity, and to allow the impetus and free flow which maintain the continuity of rolling. Down's Syndrome children usually roll even more fluently than mainstream children.

Children need encouragement to roll in a sequential way in which one part of the body follows after another. The roll may be initiated by first turning one hip, shoulder or knee, and then the rest of the body follows, involving rotation, a twist in the trunk. The body can then roll in a flexible, fluent, sequential way. One of the main aims of movement activities is to educate the centre of the body (body awareness), which is so often unknown and rigid. Flexibility in the trunk indicates that the child is sensitive to and aware of his or her body.

To help achieve flexibility in the trunk, the adult can sit with the child lying across his or her thighs, and can then roll the child down to the ankles and back up to the thighs again. The child's body moulds itself against the adult's legs and will be slightly open when he or she is on the back and slightly closed when on the stomach. The adult uses his or her body to feed sensations into the child's trunk. The adult can then lie back and roll the child right up to his or her chin and then, coming up into the sitting position, all the way down to the feet. A trusting, confident child will roll flexibly, fluently and resiliently, adapting to the adult's body. A tense, nervous child will have to be helped to relax and allow his or her body to 'melt'.

Children who are profoundly handicapped can be helped by the adult to relax. Again in a sitting position, the adult rests the child face down across his or her thighs and gently bounces the child and pats the back. The child's solar plexus – the centre of the body – must rest on the supporter's thighs with the child's arms and head resting on the floor. An anxious child will raise the head. The gentle bouncing induces relaxation, and the child can also be gently rocked from side to side. Children enjoy being patted up and down the spine. This comforting experience can help even the most disturbed or handicapped children (and adults) to relax and to accept new experiences.

The caregiver can do a double roll, holding the child along the length of the body, face to face. The adult has to be careful not to squash the child when he or she is on top, but children enjoy a double roll and like being slightly squashed. They also like being hugged, held and supported during the roll.

Children enjoy rolling other people and this is one of the easiest ways of encouraging children to move an older partner because they do not have to contend with too much weight (Fig. 7). The older partner can help the child to be successful in rolling him or her without the child being aware of this. Some disturbed children only consent to be involved with another person if they are in charge of the situation and they may exploit the situation and roll the partner roughly. As a relationship is built up and as confidence develops, the child becomes more aware of the needs of the partner and treats him or her more kindly. It is important to encourage children to take the initiative and have the experience of being in charge of the adult.

Horizontal rocking   This is a useful activity for profoundly handicapped children as it helps to reduce spasticity. The child lies on the back on a mat. The caregiver gently pulls the child up onto his or her side, handling the child on the hip and the shoulder, the bony parts of the body. The child is helped to fall back onto the back and then rolled up onto the other side. The emphasis is on the drop onto the back induced by gravity, which feeds in an experience of weight and heaviness. The free flow of rocking up on the sides and the falling back encourage relaxation. Some handlers are more skilful than others in finding the best rhythm and in combining firmness with sensitivity, but these are skills that can be learnt with practice.

6 A senior boy in a school for children with severe learning difficulties supports a girl who has profound and multiple learning difficulties

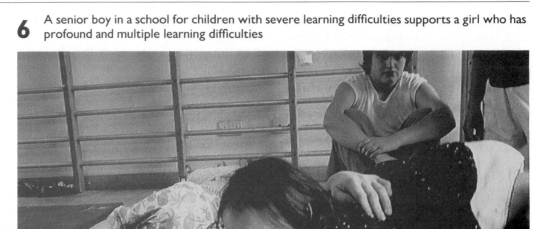

7 Day nursery. Rolling an adult

Sliding   Another caring relationship involves one partner sliding the other along a slippery floor, pulling him or her by the ankles (Figs. 8, 9). Children enjoy the experience of free-flow sliding and are surprised to see their partner above them; this activity will often produce good eye contact. The older partner can also slide the child in big sweeping movements from side to side, causing the child's waist to bend in a flexible way. The emphasis here is on the sideways movement rather than on the experience of sliding. This is another way of feeding in flexibility to the centre of the body. If the child is stiff and rigid, the caregiver knows that no new experiences are being received by the child. With care, skill and encouragement, it is possible to help children to relax and allow the centre of the body to be more flexible.

The rigidity of the trunk may extend to the legs. Tension in the legs is quite often found in the caregiver and this tension will be communicated to the child. A useful way of helping the legs to relax is for the tense person to lie down on the back. Gently, from underneath, the therapist or caregiver lifts the knee of one leg a few centimetres and lets it fall. As the leg begins to fall more easily, with less tension, the therapist lifts the leg a little higher. The emphasis is on the drop, letting gravity produce the movement. Massaging the thigh muscles can also help. Relaxed legs fall with the feet falling out sideways which indicates that the adductor muscles on the inside of the legs are relaxed. 'Worried', tense legs have the feet pointing directly upwards.

When an adult or older partner slides a child, he or she should notice if the child lets the head rest on the floor, which is a sign of self-confidence. Anxious people will lift the head and look around. If sliding is uncomfortable for the head and hair, the child can put his or her hands under the head, but this will probably not be necessary on a clean, slippery floor. Children with profound and multiple learning difficulties can be slid on a blanket; this is an enjoyable and stimulating experience for them (Fig. 10).

Children can slide adults by pulling their hands or wrists. The adults walk their feet along the floor in order to help children to pull successfully. A number of children working as a group can pull their teacher along. It is important for the children to reciprocate and look after adults.

Tunnels   In this activity the child shows initiative and independence in making use of the adult's body. Going under the adult's 'tunnel' may be the first activity in which very young, shy, children show initiative. The adult is on all fours, making a 'horse', and the child enjoys going through all the spaces made by the adult's body. The child can go under the arms, between the legs and out under the sides of the adult's body. A group of children may spontaneously start going under and through the tunnels of other adults or older children, and group play begins, a sign of security. Children particularly enjoy going through a long tunnel made by a line of adults or children (Fig. 11). Small children may also creep over and along the adults' backs.

As children crawl over the top of and underneath their partner's 'horse', their vocabulary can be increased through the physical experience of actions described as 'over', 'under', 'through', 'up', 'down',   13

8 Children with severe learning difficulties slide their partners. Note the relaxed head of the sliding girl

9 Reception class children partner a visiting class of six-year-olds

10 The seniors in a school for children with severe learning difficulties invented this method of sliding children with profound and multiple learning difficulties

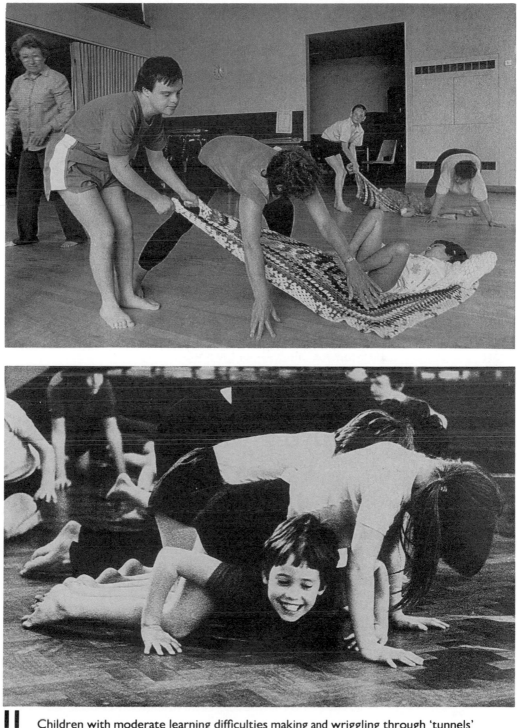

11 Children with moderate learning difficulties making and wriggling through 'tunnels'

'round', 'on top'. In fact, language is continually developed through movement play. The children enjoy the play so much that learning the meaning of words comes easily as the action and the word are experienced together.

When the child makes a tunnel for the adult, the child will have to balance on hands and feet to make a big enough space for the adult to wriggle through (see top photograph on page 76). Children enjoy seeing the adults' efforts to get through their tunnels.

More advanced support

As already stated, when a child gives his or her weight to the caregiver to support, this is a sign of commitment, of being willing to be involved with another person. It is often very difficult for a disturbed child to commit him- or herself, so the caregiver has to find ways of achieving this commitment that are not threatening to the child. For example, a child in water may not be aware of being supported because of the unfamiliar situation. Some adolescents will not let anyone touch them, but they can be encouraged to allow themselves to be supported by seeing, then imitating, other children around them who are participating in and enjoying the activities.

In this situation it is best to begin with partial support as in cradling, but there are several ways of giving full support which are not threatening. The adult can curl up, face down, and the child is then encouraged to slither over and across the back like a seal. Children also enjoy slithering over the adult's body from hips to head. The child experiences his or her body against the body of the adult.

Balancing on a partner

Children also enjoy balancing on an adult. The simplest form of this, for very young children, is for the adult to sit on the floor with legs stretched out. The child stands on the adult's thighs with hands supported, or can, daringly, balance without support.

Children enjoy balancing on the adult's body in different ways. The flow of movement here is controlled or bound, in contrast to the free flow experienced in cradling, sliding and rolling. Children enjoy standing on the adult's knees when the adult is sitting on the floor with the knees bent up. The child puts a foot on each knee and is helped to balance by holding the adult's hands, often managing to balance without help (Fig. 12). Good eye contact is usually made in this activity and the child focuses attention in a way which may not be typical of that child. All activities that help the child to focus attention, even if only for a short time, give the child practice in the necessary ability to concentrate.

Gripping

The adult can lie face down on the floor and the child is encouraged to sit astride the back. Gently the adult does little humping movements. When the child is ready the adult can rise up onto all fours making a 'horse'. The child is encouraged to grip with the legs and to hold on with arms round the adult's neck (Fig. 13). The adult can sway gently forwards and backwards, and then subside onto the ground again. If the child's grip is secure, the adult can carefully move forward on all fours and give the child a ride. Children under eighteen months are not able to grip securely but older children can learn. Gripping with arms and legs is a

12 Parents and mainstream children. Balancing. Note the eye contact and concentration

13 Nurture group for children with special needs. Clinging on with arms and legs

positive indication that the child is prepared to be involved with another person.

Children also enjoy the game of 'baby monkeys'. The adult sits in a sideways position (both legs to one side). The child sits facing the adult astride the adult's lap with legs gripping round the adult's waist and with arms round the adult's neck. The adult leans forward and comes up onto all fours with the child clinging on underneath the adult's body. The adult can put one arm around the child to help the child to cling on. This activity can only be done for a short time as it requires a lot of strength to cling on against the pull of gravity. Children enjoy the experience, and participation in this activity is a clear indication that the child wants to be in contact with the adult (Fig. 14).

Balancing on a partner's back   A child can also balance on all fours on an adult's back when the adult is already on all fours (Fig. 15). Children often extend themselves and kneel up, and some will eventually stand on the adult's back (Fig. 16). They must be asked to put one foot on the shoulders and one foot on the hips and not to stand on the adult's waist. The adult can sense how confident the child is and can sway very slightly so that the child has to concentrate to maintain balance.

Another way in which the adult can give the child support from an all-fours position is as follows. The child sits on the adult's hips, facing the adult's feet, and lies back with his or her back lying along the adult's back with the head lying over the adult's shoulder or resting on his or her head. In this position the child's body is relaxed and open. The adult can sway gently forwards and back. To help the child to get off, the adult can subside onto the floor and roll the child off sideways.

In order to take the weight of adolescents or adults, three, four or five people can kneel on all fours side by side close together, their backs making a new 'floor'. The person who is going to be carried spreads him- or herself face down to lie along all the backs (Fig. 17). The supporters together sway gently forwards and back. This commitment to the support of a group of people is significant for older people who are not used to being carried. The one who is carried can lie face up; while this is a more vulnerable position, it results in better relaxation than when lying face down. The supporters can deposit their load by each one putting an arm round the person, sitting back on their heels, and slowly and carefully unrolling the person backwards over their hips. The person who is being helped to roll off puts out an arm and a leg to help take the weight and make the landing as soft and as comfortable as possible.

Aeroplanes   This is another form of support which is much enjoyed by children. The adult lies face up with legs bent up supporting the child's stomach and legs along the shins, and holding the child on the shoulders. The child is above the adult, facing down, and this is probably the best position there is for gaining eye contact. The child feels that he or she is in a flying position. Very young children enjoy 'crash landing', when the adult lets the child drop onto his or her stomach. Some children will try lying backwards over the adult. Children are very inventive and will find many variations of such activities.

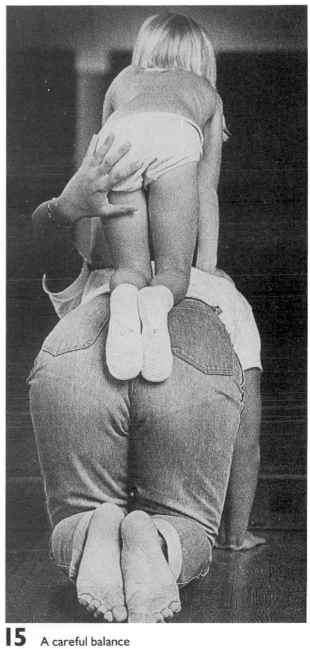

14 Mainstream 'baby monkeys' cling onto their parents against gravity

15 A careful balance by a mainstream child

16 A boy with moderate learning difficulties balances on his teacher. Note the position of the feet, and the concentration

17 Emotionally and behaviourally disturbed boys supporting and trusting each other

Somersaults   See page 8 for an activity involving a backward somersault. A forward somersault can also be very useful in many ways. The adult sits on the floor, legs stretched out and a little apart. The child stands behind one of the adult's shoulders, leans over and rests his or her stomach on the adult's shoulder. The child puts hands on the floor between the adult's legs. The adult enfolds the child's head and trunk, rounding the back and ensuring that the child lands on his or her shoulders and unrolls the spine along the floor. The child's knees and nose are kept close together so that the child is curled up throughout the somersault. The child trusts his or her weight to the adult. He or she cannot see, so has to 'listen' to what is going on in the body, learns to curl up, and develops the control necessary to transfer weight through the spine, so often an unknown part of the body (Fig. 18). Children love being upside down, and come back for repeated somersaults. They do not notice that they have been hugged during the process; it is easy to make many friends through this activity. Some children are rigid and, having no feeling of a centre, will open out; the adult will have to mould the child's body over his or her own body. Some children are tense and feel as if they have swallowed a ruler; the aim is to melt this tension. Simpler ways of developing a sense of the centre of the body will be discussed in Chapter 2.

Very young children will somersault and unroll along the adult's thighs. Agile children enjoy doing a backward somersault, having completed the forward somersault. From a sitting position between the adult's legs (back to the adult), the child can swing vigorously backwards, push hard with hands on the floor, and hips and legs will fly over the adult's shoulder. After a lot of heaving and handling the child finishes up standing behind the adult where he or she began the forward somersault. If adolescents or adults try this activity, two extra helpers are needed, one on each side, to look after the somersaulter's hips and help maintain a curled-up forward roll.

Mutual hug   All the activities described so far take place close to the floor. In this activity, the adult stands, feet firmly placed on the floor and apart, knees a little flexed, arms held out. The child takes a run at the adult and leaps onto his or her waist, gripping tightly round the waist with the legs and with arms round the neck. The adult hugs the child strongly and gives the child a swing round. This activity is popular because it is a bit risky and the free-flow spin-round is exciting. The child grips the adult and the adult grasps the child in a mutual hug. Some children have to be helped to grip because their legs hang limply down. Learning to grip can be learnt first in safer, less demanding ways, for example by playing 'baby monkeys' or 'horses' (see page 18). This is a useful activity for the end of a movement session when confidence and trust have developed between child and adult. Unfortunately it cannot be done with heavy children and adolescents unless the adults are very strong.

Jumping   Until now the emphasis has been on being supported, and on learning to fall and roll. The time comes when children need to defeat gravity and learn to contend with it. Young mainstream children will risk leaving the security of the ground in a jump on their own between the ages of two and

18   An emotionally and behaviourally disturbed boy performs a forward somersault over his house parent

Boys from a comprehensive school help a girl with moderate **19** learning difficulties to jump high

three, usually in a jump down from a step. All children can benefit from a supported jump. The partners face each other, the older partner supporting the younger by holding him or her under the elbows. The younger child holds onto the supporter's forearms. The child bounces gently with feet together and can then be bounced round the supporting partner so that the child does not come down on the spot from which he or she took off. Confident, able children can do a flying leap from one foot, landing on the other halfway round their partners. They develop a flexible free-flow way of leaping with freedom, using the knees and hip joints to make 'flying legs'.

Jumping high can be done in groups of three. Two helpers stand one on each side of the person who is going to jump. They support under the elbows and take a 'how-do-you-do' grasp of the hands. With a loud cry of 'and hup', the middle person bends his or her knees and leaps up into the air, pushed higher by the supporters, and achieves height which could not be reached unaided. Before doing this the one who is jumping needs to loosen the ankles with small bouncing jumps to ensure that the feet and ankles are resilient and ready for the landing. The one who jumps always comes down with a different face from the one he or she went up with! The free flow, the height and the exhilaration always surprise people and cheer them up (Fig. 19).

Another less demanding aspect of jumping can be developed when one partner lies on the ground spread out in a star pattern. The other partner steps over the limbs into the spaces between the limbs, and over the trunk, if this is felt to be safe. The next stage is to do a little jump over the limbs, then to leap over the partner's stomach. Some children with moderate learning difficulties will successfully leap the full length of their partner from between the legs to the farther side of the head (Fig. 20). Roles are reversed so that the other partner has the same experience of being vulnerable on the floor. This activity catches the interest of children with severe learning difficulties, and they are careful not to tread on the partner.

Transfer of weight from feet to hands

Older children and adolescents can use the body of a partner to get elevation. The supporter is on all fours. The child puts his or her hands on the adult's shoulders and hips. It is important not to put weight on the supporter's waist as it is not constructed to support weight. The child does a few small jumps with feet together, thus transferring weight to the hands, the beginning of vaulting. Children with severe learning difficulties need to have this activity demonstrated, but they enjoy attempting it. Gradually the jumps become higher and springier. When the youngsters have succeeded in getting their hips high, the next stage is to encourage them to jump round the back of their partner and land on the other side. This involves separating the legs, getting height and lift from the knees and hips, and twisting the body, almost the beginning of a cartwheel (Fig. 21). Young adults and adolescents who have severe learning difficulties can partner each other in this activity. Skilful children will perform a cartwheel over their partners, or a through vault, their legs coming between their arms as they jump from one side to the other of their support-   23

20 A mainstream boy jumps the full length of a student teacher

21 Primary school boys partner each other

ing partner. Others will leapfrog. All these activities are experiences in weight management.

Swinging   Leaving the ground can be threatening for children who are lacking in self-confidence, but the free-flow sensation of being swung is usually very much enjoyed. The easiest swing for young children is for two older people to take the child by a wrist and ankle each. The grasp of the wrist is ideally a double grasp, with each person holding the other's wrist. Hands and fingers alone are slippery and the grasp is not so secure. Between them the older people swing the child gently headwards and footwards a few times and then put the child down. As confidence develops they can take the child higher with the emphasis on taking the head high. As the child gains confidence they can take the child really high until the child is almost vertical. They drop the child's feet and the child lands on his or her feet. The moment of suspension before the landing is much enjoyed; it is near to flying (Fig. 22).

There are some children who crave free-flow, risky sensations and will demand to be swung as high as possible. In order to 'anchor' these hyperactive children, it is best for one adult to take the child by one ankle and one wrist and sweep the child around in a circle with the child's back sliding over the floor. In this way the child derives the free-flow sensation but is grounded at the same time.

When swinging adolescents or adults, four supporters are needed, one for each limb. The grasps for the arm are a double wrist-grip and a grasp above the elbow, and for the leg one grasp on the ankle and the other under the knee. People are very surprised when they are swung for the first time. They are in the power and care of four people and have to trust and commit themselves to these supporters. The sensation of swinging is so enjoyable that children and adolescents usually demand another swing.

This activity is best done towards the end of a session and will be a high-light of the session. It is quite difficult to calm everyone down after a swing unless the preceding activities have physically extended and satisfied them. The caring, 'with' activities must therefore be balanced with 'against' activities which demand strength and energy. (See '*Against' relationships* below.) A good balance between 'caring' and 'against' activities results in a sense of well-being and pleasant exhaustion.

Shared relationships

Rowing the boat   The simplest shared activity is one in which partners sit on the floor facing each other, legs outstretched. The legs of one partner may have to lie on top of the legs of the other. Very young children can sit on the older part-ner's legs. The partners grasp each other's wrists and in the case of very small children the older partner can hold the elbows. Each partner takes it in turn to lie back and then sit up and lean forward while the other partner lies back on the floor (Fig. 23).

There are two aims to this activity. One is to help the child lie back so that his or her head rests on the ground, a sign of confidence. The other   25

22 A hearing-impaired child enjoys a high swing

23 Children with severe learning difficulties in a hospital school 'rowing the boat'. Note the relaxed head on the floor

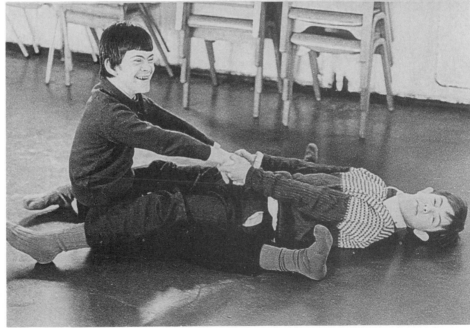

aim is to encourage the child to pull the older partner back up into a sitting position again when it is the older partner's turn to sit up. The adult ensures that the child is successful in doing this by unobtrusively assisting the child if necessary. The adult also observes the strength and determination of the child's pulling action. At one moment the child is higher than the adult, and the next the adult is higher. Eye contact is usually made at these points. In this activity, partners alternately support each other and pull each other, and the child demonstrates confidence in the partner and in him- or herself and contributes to the shared activity.

Balancing with a partner   A shared balance, which is more demanding, can be tackled by mainstream children and by adolescents with special needs. Partners sit on the floor facing each other, knees bent and feet apart in a stable position. The partners grasp each other's wrists and, pulling hard, manage to stand up together (Fig. 24). The distance between them will be adjusted to the length of their arms, which are slightly flexed. Partners can then sit down together, balancing each other's weight. They need to keep their hips underneath them and not let them protrude backwards as this makes the partners much heavier and more difficult to balance. This activity can be started from a standing position. Partners take up a firm stance with feet apart, grasp wrists, and lean back so that they get used to the experience of depending on another person while at the same time holding that person up. Children with severe learning difficulties find it threatening to be off-balance, they want to be stable, but through a comprehensive movement programme they can learn to relate in a mutually dependent, mutually supportive way.

Balancing a partner requires a great deal of sensitive awareness of the other person, while at the same time being in control of the weight-bearing parts of one's own body. Balancing also demands controlled flow, the opposite of free-flowing movement. This means that the action is under the control of the will; it also calls on all the concentration of the two people involved and on their ability to 'listen' to each other. This capacity to listen to and relate can be developed in caregivers. If the centre of the body and the weight-bearing legs and hips are well controlled, the caregiver can give all his or her attention to the child. A heavier adult can balance a lighter child if the adult has sufficient control over his or her own weight, so that the adult gives the child only as much weight to support as the child can manage.

See-saws   Agile, well-coordinated children enjoy making a see-saw. One child rises as the other child sinks. They also enjoy sitting back to back, knees bent and with a stable base. They push so hard against each other's backs that they stand up together (Fig.25). They balance with the whole spine in contact with the other person, and then sit down together. This activity requires strong thigh muscles and sensitive cooperation between partners. Children also enjoy an upside-down balance. They lie down on their backs, bottoms touching, legs in the air, holding each other's wrists. They press their feet hard against their partner's feet, lift their feet off the floor and make an arch with their bodies, balancing on their shoulders (Fig. 26).

24 Profoundly deaf children balance the weight of a partner. Note the concentration

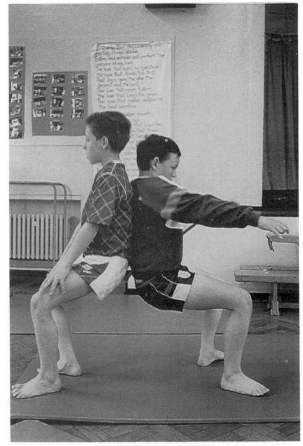

25 Middle school boys do a back-to-back balance standing and sitting, keeping spines in contact

Children also enjoy a balance standing on an adult's thighs (or those of an older partner). The adult stands facing the child, knees flexed and feet apart. He or she grasps the child's wrists and the child steps up onto the adult, one foot on each thigh. If the child is small the adult may hold onto the elbows. The child leans back, as does the adult, and they perform a spectacular balance (Fig. 27).

Balancing can be experienced by groups of three, four or five people standing in a circle. The controlled flow and the sensitive awareness involved is enjoyed more by adults than by children. The children enjoy the more athletic balances, many of which they invent.

It will be noticed that when children balance, whether it is a shared balance with another person or kneeling on a partner's back, they give their full attention to the activity. Attention spans can be increased if the motivation is strong enough. A great deal of the necessary concentration is caught, or picked up, from the adult. The tone of voice and steady eye contact help a child to concentrate. The child is also more motivated to be involved in activities if the older partner is also enjoying and sharing in the movement play.

Another shared relationship, which has already been described (see page 21), is the mutual hug.

'Against' relationships

When a child has received movement experiences from an older partner in caring or 'with' relationships and has begun to show initiative and to instigate relationship play, the child is ready to experience relationships against the older partner. This readiness may take some months to achieve in the case of very young children, children with severe learning difficulties, or emotionally damaged children. 'Against' relationships will be much enjoyed in early sessions by confident, active children. They may also provide the only way of reaching some disturbed, hyperactive and aggressive children who find that sensitive, caring experiences are threatening, and may initially only accept relationship play if it is exciting and vigorous. In an 'against' relationship the child tests his or her strength against that of the older partner. The older partner adjusts to the strength of the child, and the child develops controlled strength through these activities.

The aim of 'against' relationships is to help the child to focus and canalise energy and to develop determination. It is important for the child to discover and learn to control his or her own strength and to learn to use that strength in an appropriate way, neither exerting too much nor, on the other hand, exerting too little strength or none at all. The task of the older partner is not to dominate and win battles of strength but to 'feed in' experiences of strength to the younger partner. The older partner tests the younger, encouraging effort, and allowing the child to be successful only as a result of using all the energy and effort of which the child is capable. This may be very little or a great deal. There are some adults who find it difficult to allow children to be successful against them. The child must be successful but should be encouraged to work for it. It is essential that 'against' relationships are humorous and are treated as play.

29

26 Children with moderate learning difficulties balance upside down

27 A spectacular balance by emotionally and behaviourally disturbed boys

One of the main problems for children with special needs is the inability to concentrate and so to learn from experience. If children learn to use their strength in a focused way, especially along direct, linear pathways, they will develop skills in attending, in directing their energy and concentrating on a job. As a child learns to direct attention to tasks which are enjoyable and rewarding, he or she will be more able to focus attention on activities which are less immediately attractive. Research has shown that children are more able to relate to each other and are more able to focus attention on tasks in the classroom after a movement lesson than when they have not had a movement class.

Squashing the child   The adult lies on top of and across the body of the child on the floor. The child is encouraged to wriggle out from underneath the adult's body (Fig. 28). The adult only rests as much weight on the child as the child can cope with, and the child experiences great satisfaction and a sense of achievement on escaping; the child also enjoys the sensation of being squashed. The adult feeds in an experience of strength and determination.

Rocks   Other 'against' activities combine strength with stability and are enjoyed by both mainstream and handicapped children. The adult can help a child to be firm and stable in a sitting position on the floor, knees bent up, feet apart (this is essential as feet together do not provide a firm base), hands with fingers spread out and firmly fixed on the floor. The child is a 'rock'. The adult tests this 'rock' by pushing gently on the knees. If the child's body braces against the pressure, the adult can push a little harder, but must not push the child off his or her base. The adult approaches the child from the front in a controlled way, moving on a direct pathway to help create an atmosphere of concentration. Here the voice can help and the adult's attitude can increase the child's sense of firmness and stability. Eye contact is also direct and concentrated. The adult then tests from the back on the shoulders. Again the child braces against the pressure and calls up strength, particularly in the trunk and legs. The adult begins with very light pressure, increasing it as the child's strength develops. The aim is to give the child an experience of firmness and stability, and not to destroy this.

When it comes to the adult's turn to make a 'rock' and to be tested by the child, the adult encourages the child to push hard on the knees. When the adult feels the child has used all his or her strength, the adult falls over, to the child's great delight.

When working with children with severe learning difficulties who have virtually no concept of strength, the adult should sit beside the child, put one of the child's hands on the adult's shoulder and say 'push'. The adult may need to help the child's arm to push. The adult should promptly fall over. Thus the child is rewarded and will make more of an effort next time. Pushing something away, and kicking with the feet, are actions which are seen early in young children. Doing something to a person is a necessary experience for children who are passive, and this activity may be the first indication that the child has some initiative.

31

28 Day nursery. Wriggling out from underneath a nursery nurse

29 Profoundly deaf children test stability and strength in a back-to-back push

Back to back   There is a variety of ways in which children can test each other's stability and strength and thus feed these experiences in to each other. The simplest one is for two children to sit back to back, knees bent up. They stick their feet into the ground in a firm, wide base in front of them, and their hands stick to the floor behind them. They then push backwards against each other and see how strong their partner is; the result is usually a static battle (Fig. 29). When adults try this, there is always a great deal of laughter, a reaction to the great output of effort. When older mainstream children work with younger children, they soon understand the concept of testing and not winning, and realise that they are developing strength in their partners.

One variation of this activity is enjoyed by all children. Partners sit back to back; one partner is the 'engine', who gives the other partner a slide, or ride, over the floor. The 'engine' has to work hard pushing with hands and feet against the floor, while the partner who is having the ride bends the knees so as to give the least friction against the floor. He or she also walks the feet along the ground. The aim is to travel as fast as possible and the one who is pushed can steer. Roles are then reversed. When a larger partner is pushed by a smaller partner, the larger can help the smaller by propelling him- or herself along the ground with hands as well as feet so that the younger partner is successful in the pushing action.

A relationship through the back is non-threatening and is often more acceptable than a face-to-face relationship. It is comfortable, and it is easy to make friends with shy children through back-to-back rides.

There are three positions in which the body can be experienced as firm, stable and unmovable. These positions explore the body's power to stick to the floor. We have already considered the 'rock' in a sitting position. In a second position, one partner lies face down, spreadeagled on the floor, holding the ground, expressing the idea 'I shall not be moved'. The other partner kneels at one side and attempts to push the partner off his or her base by pushing or pulling on the shoulder and hip. It is virtually impossible to move anyone who is determined and strong. The aim is to confirm the partner's stability and not to destroy it. There is great concentration of physical strength as well as mental concentration of both partners. Children can use the back to push the partner with, or the top of the head, or the feet. When the child pushes the adult, the adult should allow the child to be successful by rolling over. Lying face down is a stronger position than lying face up, but lying face up has the advantage that the opponents can see each other and enjoy the fun involved.

The third stable position is on all fours with one leg extended sideways, foot on the floor, which acts as an added stabiliser. This tent-like anchored position can be tested from all angles – back, front, and both sides. The tester must give preparatory warning where the pressure is to be exerted by putting hands firmly on the body and starting to push gently at first. It is an interesting experience to feel the body brace against pressure and acquire organised strength. It is possible to feed in intelligent use of energy so that the person who is tested gains greater mastery and control over the body. (See Figs. 30 and 31.)

30 Children with severe learning difficulties. Testing a 'rock'. The girl is stable, but the boy has little awareness of strength

31 Middle school girls. Testing a 'rock' and displaying directed energy

Prisons   The simplest way to introduce strength against a partner is for the older partner to make a containing 'house', sitting on the floor with the child between the legs. The 'house', which is initially a receptive, cradling, sensitive container, becomes a 'prison' when the older partner's arms and legs squeeze and grip the child (Fig. 32). The child is encouraged to wriggle out using the 'front door' (the arms can be prised apart), the side 'windows', or out of the 'chimney'. The older partner lets the child escape while providing just enough restraining power to make the child struggle hard to escape. Most children, having escaped from their 'prison', promptly jump back inside for another battle.

Some very young children cannot understand the concept of pushing against the adult and stay inside passively. If they are held loosely and encouraged to emerge, they may do so. Some children, especially those who are socially deprived, may like being held tightly in a 'prison' so much that they have no wish to escape from this pleasant and probably unfamiliar security.

In the case of energetic and perhaps emotionally disturbed children, the battle to get out of the adult's restraining 'prison' is much enjoyed and provides a safe and vigorous exchange between adult and child. It is a paradox, but 'against' relationships often strengthen physical and psychological contact between adult and child. There is a strong element of play, of rough and tumble and of drama in this type of activity. So much depends on the older partner's estimation of the determination and strength of the younger partner. If escape is too easy it is unsatisfying.

When working with adolescents or adults, those who make the 'prison' should sit behind their partner with legs round the partner's waist, crossing their ankles over their partner's stomach. They put their arms under the partner's arms and hold their own wrists. Being strongly gripped in this way often leaves the prisoners helpless, but with great effort and after a great battle the prisoners eventually escape.

There are some children who are almost impossible to hold. They manage to slide out of any grasp. They are usually highly disturbed children and an 'against' relationship of this type is not appropriate in the early stages of building a relationship.

Caregivers need to have a good relationship to their own strength; that is, they should develop their capacity to be strong and to use this strength in a positive way, should the need arise. They should learn to control this strength and adapt it to the needs of other people in relationship play activities. They also need to be able to use the opposite aspects of energy – sensitivity and fine touch – when it is appropriate. Children instinctively know if the adult has a good relationship to his or her own strength. Many more women than men work both with mainstream children and in special education, and it is essential that they develop this awareness of their own strength.

Boys particularly enjoy the testing of their strength and the rough and tumble of 'prisons'. The teacher has to balance a programme so that the 'against' relationships are interspersed with caring or 'with' experiences. Boys and girls both need experiences of being strong and stable as well as those of being gentle and free flowing. The balancing of opposites is important.

35

32   An older boy with moderate learning difficulties makes a 'prison' for a younger child in his school

2

Developing body awareness

Early development

Significance of early learning experiences

Babies receive movement experiences from their parents or caregivers, who feed in both physical and emotional security as they handle the young child. A confident, experienced caregiver will communicate trustworthiness, competence, sensitivity and awareness of the baby's needs. In handling people of any age, the aim is to be both firm and sensitive. This may seem a paradox, but the firmness induces confidence in the recipient and indicates that the handler is confident in what he or she is doing; sensitivity is experienced as the handler's sympathetic adaptation of the activity to the particular needs of the recipient. Many people are unaware of the messages they are conveying when they handle children, particularly to young babies who are passive recipients and can do very little for themselves.

This sensitivity requires the caregiver to put him- or herself into the situation of the very young child, to anticipate what the child will experience and to make the experience as pleasant and as acceptable as possible. The caregiver needs to accompany activities with a warm supportive voice, talking, humming or singing. Gentle, rhythmical bouncing is comforting, as is gentle swaying from side to side.

Many parents and caregivers have to *learn* how to handle their first baby. In the not-so-distant past, children in large families looked after their younger brothers and sisters, but these days it is quite likely that a mother has never handled a baby until she has her first child. If she is nervous about handling her baby, this will be communicated to the child. The inexperienced parent has to learn on the first child. The parent, or anyone else, handling a young, physically handicapped child, is understandably nervous and is often tentative and anxious about harming the child. All young children feel safer if they are handled firmly and confidently. The adult has to develop this confidence through practice and experience. If the adult has had personal experience of confident, warm handling as a child, this is likely to be passed on. In movement sessions for profoundly and multiply handicapped children, it is easy to identify those caregivers who have brought up children or who are 37 physiotherapists. Their confidence, firmness and sensitivity are transmitted to the children. Some people are more skilled than others at creating a rapport with children.

In the early stages the baby is supported, dressed, undressed, contained, carried, bathed, cradled and played with, and the way in which all these activities are carried out will be an important part of the baby's first experiences.

Containing and cradling are whole body movements which feed in to the child his or her totality and weightiness, and have a harmonious effect on the child. The more the baby's body is in contact with the parent's or caregiver's body, the better. The baby who is carried on the front or the back of the adult experiences the rhythms of the adult walking, working, and generally moving about. The child benefits from the sensory stimulus of the adult's movement as well as from the warmth of the adult's body. Physical contact and closeness are very important for the developing baby.

On the whole, babies' bodies fit into the bodies of the adults who hold and carry them. They melt and mould themselves into the adults' bodies in a flexible, resilient way. Babies who have not been held in a warm, caring way are less likely to have responsive bodies. During movement sessions such children often have tense, rigid, non-communicating and unresponsive bodies, while those who have been handled well respond readily and spontaneously to movement experiences. The early learning experiences of being safely held and contained with good feeling have a marked effect on a young child's ability to respond to human contact and to form relationships. Experience has shown that it is possible to help a mother who has had post-natal depression to play physically with her baby, so that although the baby may have suffered initially, a good rapport is eventually built up between mother and child.

Babies respond to having their bodies stroked or massaged. Some African and Asian mothers massage their babies as part of their culture, and massage can be a means of working oil into the baby's skin. In the West we do not have a tradition of massaging babies, but babies do benefit from it both sensorily and psychologically, and it is a valuable means of communicating the mother's concern for her child.

Besides stroking babies it is important to pat and tickle them. Patting and tickling can be quite strong or very gentle, adapted to the needs of the child. Feeding in physical experiences can be repeated as the child grows. It is easier to work with a child who has received physical attention of different kinds.

The baby's interaction with the parent or caregiver

All movement play is a kind of conversation. In the beginning the parent initiates the relationship and the child responds. Parents of handicapped children may find they elicit little or no response, and may feel disheartened and cease to try to stimulate their children. Handicapped children need more sensory stimulation and more attempts at building a relationship than normal children, but it is understandable that parents and caregivers lose heart if they receive no feedback or very little response.

It is important to encourage the child to focus on the adult's face, particularly on the eyes, and to enjoy and respond to a variety of sounds and noises, and language, made by the adult. This is the beginning of communication. Later the child may initiate his or her own movements and sounds; the adult needs to imitate these and feed them back to the child. The habit of making eye contact can be developed early and needs continuous reinforcement.

Some mothers are under so much stress that they are unable to play or relate to their children; they are in great need of support, and this applies particularly to parents of handicapped children. The time when these parents most need help is at the beginning.

Development of physical skills

Normal babies develop their own powers of moving their limbs. Vigorous kicking movements are seen early, and gradually the control of grasping develops. The physically handicapped baby needs to be stimulated and moved passively to try and feed into the child that he or she has a body. Every handicapped child is different, and it is essential that the family of a handicapped child has professional help from a physiotherapist so that they know how to handle and help their child from a very early age. It is important not to move the child mechanically, but to make the experience as enjoyable as possible, making the learning a play situation.

The caregivers of the handicapped child need perseverance and patience, and they need all the support and advice they can get for the treatment of the child. There is a great temptation to leave a passive, undemanding child to lie quite still all day. Some children with profound and multiple learning difficulties go to schools for children with severe learning difficulties, and may function as if they were a few months old. There is a great need for teachers of these children to have specialist help both in physiotherapy and in movement education, and this information should be passed on and shared with parents and caregivers. (See Chapter 6.)

Whenever possible the young baby should lie on his or her stomach with the head turned to one side. There should be no pillow. Every time the baby lifts the head to turn it, all the muscles of the back and neck are used and are gradually strengthened. It is important to develop strong back muscles in preparation for sitting. Later, if the baby is continually propped up against a pillow, he or she will develop a weak, rounded spine and will find sitting up straight difficult. Being able to sit securely is an important developmental achievement, as then the child's hands and arms are free to reach for and handle all kinds of objects, and hand/eye skills can develop. Sitting is also important for the development of skills involved in eating, chewing and swallowing. The muscles used for chewing food are also the muscles involved in the development of speech. Early on it is advisable to encourage a baby to lift the head from a prone position so as to develop the back muscles.

The next stage of movement against the pull of gravity is for the baby, in   39 a lying position, face down, to push with the arms and raise the top of the body off the floor. The baby will do this partly to see better, and this is the beginning of achieving a position on all fours, preparatory to crawling. It is fascinating to watch a young child experimenting with the ways of coping with the weight of the body. Having pushed the chest off the floor, the child then sits back on his or her heels, supporting the body on the hands and knees. When the child achieves a position on all fours, he or she sways unsteadily. The normal child will discover for him- or herself how to crawl; the handicapped child can be helped to achieve a position on all fours and encouraged to make the first efforts at crawling. (See Chapter 6.)

An earlier form of locomotion discovered by some babies is to roll from one place to another. It is useful to teach a baby to roll over; this can be done by placing an arm or a leg across the body when the baby is lying on the back and pulling it gently. Eventually the baby will learn to turn the rest of the body. With encouragement the baby can learn to turn onto the back again. Adventurous babies will explore a room by rolling. It is advisable to encourage the baby to crawl rather than to let the child use a method of locomotion that is sometimes seen, where the child uses one leg to propel the body forward in a sitting position, while the other leg is tucked underneath. This is because it is better if both legs develop equally in a crawling action. Many people consider that crawling is an important stage in development because it involves the coordination of all four limbs and use of the limbs on opposite sides of the body. Crawling also involves balance and management of the weight of the body, and helps to develop body awareness. However, the method of travelling on the bottom is necessary for children who are visually handicapped. They need to be able to feel what is in front of them with their hands so that they don't hit objects with their head.

Babies love to stand on their parents' thighs and kick against the thighs of the adult, just as they enjoy kicking when they are lying in a cot. This pushing against the adult and extending the knee joints should be encouraged because by doing so the child is strengthening the thigh muscles, in preparation for taking the weight of the body when standing. Any activity which helps the child strengthen thigh muscles is helpful. Taking weight on the long bones of the legs also encourages the bony tissue at the end of the long bones to be strengthened and to grow. When the baby eventually pulls him- or herself into a standing position, the muscles of the legs will be well prepared to take weight. Every step in development can thus be prepared for beforehand.

Normal children are geared towards defeating gravity in learning to sit, crawl, stand and walk; to a large extent they will teach themselves to develop these skills. The handicapped child will experience varying degrees of difficulty in acquiring these skills and will need a great deal of encouragement and, ideally, professional help from a physiotherapist or an experienced teacher.

Pre-school children and school children

It is most important that children become aware of their own bodies. Many writers have discussed the concept of body awareness, and it is interesting to note the different ways of describing this: body concept; body image; body consciousness, body sense; body schema.

On the whole, physical education teaches children to perform skills in manipulating objects such as balls, beanbags, hoops, bats, etc. and to develop skills in relation to movement on large apparatus, climbing frames, slides, swings, etc. These skills which we might refer to as 'objective skills', are valuable to the child and have an important place in education. However, in this book we are concerned with a 'subjective' approach to movement education; that is, with developing awareness of the body. Both approaches to education are necessary; the child should be aware of his or her own body, and learn too how to handle objects and how to cope with the external world. The child needs both 'objective' and 'subjective' skills. Much has been written about acquiring objective skills of all kinds and about the development of hand/eye coordination. Here we are concerned with the development of body awareness.

Movement of the body as a whole

It is important to feed in a sense of wholeness to the child and not concentrate only on movement of separate parts of the body. Whole body movement involving the free flow of weight has a harmonious effect on all children. Wholeness is experienced particularly in rolling on the floor, where weight is used to facilitate the roll. It is also experienced in all forms of bouncing, which can, in addition, be a calming activity. On a trampoline or trampette the child experiences the full weight of the body against the bed of the trampoline and learns to use weight in a positive way. The child may bounce in a standing or a sitting position. Any work on a trampoline must of course be supervised by a qualified instructor, as it can be dangerous.

Sliding is another free-flow experience of the whole body which is enjoyed by children, whether along the floor or down a slide. Swinging on a swing changed the mood of one highly disturbed eight-year-old girl in a school for children with moderate learning difficulties. After twenty minutes on a swing she would calm down and was able to work in the classroom without attacking other people. Swimming, and playing in water, also have a calming and harmonising effect on children.

Awareness of the weight-bearing parts of the body

It is essential, wherever possible, to help children to develop skills in locomotion of all kinds. Children should be able to stand, run and jump, and be able to take part in a variety of sports, dance, and outdoor activities. If the lower half of the body is well educated, the upper half will look after itself; it is essential to develop a well-functioning basic structure.

On the whole, movement of the non-weight-bearing extremities and the feet are well covered in physical education programmes and in hand/eye activities in the classroom. Children are aware of their feet and hands, parts of themselves which they can easily see and move, but they have to be helped to become aware of their knees and hips. Many children with severe learning difficulties have little control of the weight-bearing parts of their bodies and walk with a wide gait in an effort to maintain balance. Caregivers should concentrate on developing awareness of parts of the body that are not easily seen, of which the child is often unaware, and which play a significant part in all movement.

Awareness of knees
Children of all ages, those with special needs and mainstream children, benefit from activities that help them to become more aware of their knees. The knees are the 'halfway house' between the hips and the feet. They are the most important joints for controlling movement of the body in standing, walking, running, jumping, landing, being stable, changing direction, sitting down and standing up. The muscle which controls the knee joint, helping to hold the joint firmly and to extend it, is the quadriceps muscle, the four heads of which extend from the pelvis to the kneecap and into the front of the tibia. If the knee joint is damaged, the muscle tone is lost quite quickly in the thigh muscle and this has to be built up to make the knee joint secure again.

When working with younger children and children with special needs, it is helpful to begin the process of knee awareness by sitting on the floor so that the legs are not bearing weight and can move freely. The children hold onto their knees so that they can feel what is happening to them. They bend their knees up and press them down to straighten their legs out. This is called 'the disappearing knee trick'. Children find many humorous ways of making their knees bend and disappear again. They can, in mime, 'pump up' one knee and prick it with a pin; they can 'wind up' one knee, or pull it up with a thread, and cut the thread. There are many variations on this, some of which the children will find for themselves. For example, still holding onto their knees the children press their bent knees together and then separate them as far as they will go sideways, still bent. They hammer their bent knees with their fists, enjoying the sound. They smack their bent knees, noticing the different sound this makes. They rub their knees and tickle them lightly. The knees should sting a bit as a result of all the hammering and smacking, which helps the children to realise they have got bony knees. The children knock their elbows on their knees and cross them over to touch the opposite knee, crossing the mid-line of the body. They can join their chin to the knee and the nose to the knee. It is useful to feel bone on bone and to join children up to themselves.

Weight bearing
The next stage is perhaps rather painful for adults but children enjoy it. The children kneel up on their knees; this may be the first time they have taken weight on them. They can walk on their knees or slide on them using their hands on the floor to propel themselves along. They can

change direction moving backwards and sideways as well as forwards, and they can turn round. These experiences help the children to retain awareness of their knees even though they are now bearing weight and are difficult to see.

Shutting and opening Children enjoy other forms of travel or locomotion that make them aware of their knees and elbows. They curl up, face down, on the floor with their knees and elbows touching on each side. They shuffle forwards with little steps, keeping their knees and elbows close together. With their heads tucked in the children feel very small and can concentrate on the experience of being close to themselves. Then they can try the 'opening/shutting' animal. They slide their elbows forwards along the floor and slide their knees backwards so that they are lying full length on their stomachs on the ground. With a sudden snap they join their knees and elbows together in a 'shut' position. In this manner they can make progress along the floor, moving forwards by bringing their knees up to their elbows. Many ways of getting about using hands and knees can be discovered and encouraged. The physical contact of the knees against the floor helps the children to experience their knees preparatory to the next stage, in which the children take weight on their feet and legs.

Little legs The children now get into a squatting position on their feet with their knees near their shoulders. They still hold onto their knees so that they do not forget them. With these 'little legs' they can walk, hop, and jump like a frog. They can move forwards, backwards, sideways, and turn round. The knees can move close together, or very wide apart. 'Little legs' are much enjoyed by children as they feel they are like creatures or little people. They are very inventive, discovering different ways of getting about, far more so than adults, who are more conventional.

The children now 'grow legs', and with their feet apart in a stable position they slowly extend their knees until they are almost standing, but with slightly flexed knees. They can also 'grow legs' in a series of small jerking movements like a puppet. Now that weight is taken on the legs it is easy to forget about the knees so the children still hold onto them and walk about using different directions and different rhythms. The knees can be stuck together or kept wide apart, and they can cross over in a scissor-like way. The children can walk or jump holding onto their knees. They can jump one knee high up sideways and then the other; they can do little jumps on both feet; they can turn around with one knee leading the turn. As they move they feel that their knees are the most important feature of their bodies.

High knees The final stage comes when the children stop holding their knees, and walk and jump. They are still aware of their knees, but now their knees can move more freely. It is useful to help the children experience 'high knees', taking one knee at a time. First the knee jumps forwards up to the chin, then one knee jumps sideways to try to touch the ear. With the child on all fours, one knee can be *lifted* high backwards. It is safer not to *jump* the knee backwards as the child could fall on the face. In this way the child discovers that the knee can be lifted high forwards, sideways and back- 43 wards, and this loosens up the hip joints and teaches the child about directions in space. So often children only jump with their feet together. Movement into space behind the child, where the knee is out of sight, may be difficult initially for children with severe learning difficulties because they cannot see where their leg is. Awareness of space behind can develop quite early, for example when a young child goes downstairs backwards, reaching for the next step.

The teacher now asks the children to run and jump with high knees. This is going against gravity, and elevation may be difficult for severely retarded children. The experience of height and jumping is a necessary contrast to body movement close to the floor. It is best not to jump off two feet and land on two feet as the jump and movement of the legs is restricted. The leap high in the air is off one foot and the landing is on the other foot so that there is a sense of flight and free flow, particularly in the flying legs. Height is achieved by the force of the knee swinging upwards, and with help from the elbows.

Having experienced elevation from the knee, the children can start to control the jumping action and become more familiar with the use of their legs to obtain height. Skipping involves elevation of the body with first one knee leading and then the other, while the supporting leg does a hop (Fig. 33). The coordination for this may be difficult at first. Galloping is enjoyed and involves the consecutive lift of each knee. The aim is to develop free-flowing experience of leaving the ground, to defeat gravity, and to retain awareness of the knees during the main part of the necessary effort.

The corollary to flying is to learn how to fall; this will be discussed later (see pages 50–2).

Expressive legs Mainstream children enjoy discovering the expressive use of their legs. They like to find out how to walk with their knees stuck together or with them kept wide apart. They particularly enjoy walking with wobbly knees, or 'jelly' knees, where they have little control over their legs and nearly fall down. This is contrasted with stiff legs with knees pressed back ('no knees'), which makes getting about difficult, or the jelly legs may be contrasted with strong, stable legs with slightly flexed knees. There is muscular control of the knee joint when the leg is flexed.

Children with severe learning difficulties find it very difficult to allow their bodies to be off balance. Many of them need a great deal of help to develop stability and to acquire a normal gait as opposed to a wide or shuffling gait, and it is not appropriate to ask them to move in an off-balance way.

Funny walks Mainstream children enjoy working with a partner who moves in an opposite kind of way: one may squat and walk with 'little legs', while the partner moves with long straight legs. Other partnerships can involve a child who has knees wide apart and is stable while the other moves with knees stuck together, or may have wobbly legs. Drama develops with one partner leading and the other following. Children are inventive and enjoy funny walks. The expressive use of legs is a hallmark of many comics and clowns.

33 Children with severe learning difficulties skip with high knees

Awareness of hips
Because the hips are central and are not easily seen, they are a difficult part of the body to become aware of.

All children like spinning on their bottoms on a slippery floor. They push themselves round with their hands and enjoy the free-flow spin. It is useful to suggest that at the end of their spin they fall over. It is likely that one child will do this by accident and the teacher will pick this up and ask all the children to try it. It is important that children can fall with confidence in a relaxed and fluent way, so that the experience is not painful. Older children can 'walk' on their hip bones, though this can be painful for thin people.

Children can also become more aware of their hips by lying on their backs with their knees bent up and feet firmly placed on the floor, a little apart for stability. They lift up the hips, balancing on their shoulders and their feet, making an arch with their bodies. A partner can creep through this tunnel.

Children can be helped to become aware of their hips when they somersault over an older partner's shoulder (as described in Chapter 1). The older partner sits, legs stretched out, and the child stands behind the partner. The child feels the spine unrolling along the floor or mat and should be aware of the hips touching the ground at the end of the somersault. When a partner rolls another child along the ground the partner should handle the child on the hip and shoulder and should be aware of the hip girdle and shoulder girdle of the other person.

The most difficult test of awareness of hips is experienced when two people balance each other in standing (see page 28). They face each other holding wrists; they are stable with feet apart and knees slightly bent with their hips kept over their heels, their base. If the pelvis swings forwards or backwards the partners will find it difficult to support each other. The ability to balance the hips over the heels is essential for many sports, particularly skiing.

Awareness of the hips is also seen in bunny jumps or crouch jumps when weight is taken on the hands and the hips are lifted up into the air. High hips are also seen when one partner makes a supporting 'horse' on all fours; the other partner places hands on the 'horse's' hips and shoulders, and jumps the hips high (see Fig. 21).

When a partner tests the stability of a child who is in a stable position or on all fours, the partner must use the whole body, including the hips (see Fig. 31). There is a tendency for the arms to push forwards while the hips extend backwards. This is an uneconomic use of strength as the tester's weight is not going with the action. Figure 30 shows a mentally handicapped boy who is unaware of his hips and knees. Children with good coordination will push, pull or hit a ball with their hips, moving in the same direction as the rest of the body; they take their hips with them. When the centre of gravity is lowered, as happens regularly in all sports and in dance, the hips, the heaviest part of the body, must be balanced over the heels and not allowed to project backwards, as this will lead to lack of control of weight. The hips and spine are the most difficult parts of the body for people to become aware of.

Awareness of the trunk

For all children, particularly young ones, the trunk is an unknown area. The trunk is the link between the extremities, and children who are unaware of their trunk will move in an empty, disconnected way. This is particularly noticeable in developmentally retarded children. A child who is aware of having a centre will move in a connected, whole way. Awareness of the trunk can be observed when children are transferring weight in rolling, tumbling and falling activities. The child experiences the front and back of the trunk against the floor, mat or gymnastic apparatus, and against the bodies of others in activities such as rolling, somersaulting, sliding and creeping.

If a child has a sensitive, mobile centre of the body, this indicates that the child is learning from bodily experiences. It indicates that new experiences are going into the child's body. This is clearly seen when a child is slid along the floor being swayed from side to side. If the waist bends from side to side in a flexible and fluent way, this indicates that the child is relaxed and that information is going into the body. It is impossible to teach new skills in body awareness if the centre is rigid. The stomach and solar plexus are particularly important areas of the trunk and cannot be separated from awareness of shoulders, back and hips.

All the activities which increase awareness of the trunk should be presented in an enjoyable way so that learning is experienced as fun. Awareness of the trunk is best developed against supportive surfaces such as the floor, because the body can move more freely when it is well supported than when the body is standing and balance is a problem. The child is not then concerned with maintaining balance and the trunk can move with greater flexibility from a spatial point of view, and develop greater mobility in all the joints.

Lateral trunk movement

The spine is often stiff and rigid, but children can be helped by learning to creep like a lizard. They should be encouraged to lie on their stomachs on the floor, with the elbow and knee of one side touching. This means that the spine is curved and is concave towards that side. The other hand reaches forwards and the other foot pushes the body forwards until the elbow and knee of the other side of the body meet and the spine bends towards that side. In this way the child creeps forward along the floor, obtaining maximum bending from side to side of the spine. This curving of the spine can be observed from above, and it is useful for a partner to stand above the creeping partner and see how the back bends.

It is possible for physically handicapped children and adults to progress over the floor in this flexible manner, even if they cannot stand. They could even creep over each other until they make a pile of people in the middle of the room. Physical awareness, independence of locomotion, and physical contact, are particularly significant for people who are constantly in wheelchairs. While creeping along the floor, eye contact is focused on other people because it is difficult to look elsewhere.

Unfortunately, not all floors are suitable for spinning, sliding and creeping. Ideally the floor should be clean, slightly slippery, and warm to the touch.

Awareness of the   If children can curl up, they are aware of having a centre to curl up to.
centre

Parcels   The simplest way to curl up is to make a 'parcel' or 'package'. The child should lie on his or her side and hug the knees. The partner can then test the child's strength in maintaining a curled-up parcel by pulling gently on the child's limbs – if the child is young or only has a little strength – or pulling vigorously if the child is strong. It is essential not to succeed in opening the parcel; the aim is for the child to develop strength by resisting being opened out.

Many children with severe learning difficulties have little or no awareness of a centre and will have to be helped to curl up. An adult can hug and contain a child to give the child an experience of being curled up in a ball shape and close to him- or herself. Being curled up and centred rather than extending into space is important because movement into space must come from a 'home', a centre, for it to have any meaning. One often sees children in dance sessions and in gymnastics who move in an empty and disconnected way; the movement is peripheral and does not grow from the centre. Once the centre has been experienced then movement into space has some meaning.

Children can experience what it is like to make a parcel by trying to open a parcel made by the teacher. The teacher lies on his or her back, hugging the knees. The children pull at the teacher's arms and legs (not more than eight at a time!), and the teacher slowly allows the group to be successful in opening him or her out, making sure that the children have to work hard in doing so.

A stronger test of the ability to maintain the centre can be tried with more able children. The children curl up face down on the floor and the adult lifts up each child, holding them under the chest and waist. The children keep curled up against gravity; they keep their 'undercarriage' in position while being lifted up (Fig. 34). It is only possible to do this with relatively light children between the ages of three and seven. Children enjoy this and have a sense of achievement. If children come 'undone', one should go back to testing them lying sideways and curled up on the floor.

It is a good idea to work on 'parcels' before attempting somersaults, as children develop the skill of keeping their noses near their knees and keeping their bodies curled up. This means that when they attempt somersaults they will not open out but will keep their bodies in a ball shape throughout the somersault.

It is interesting to compare the ability of a mainstream child of three or four to maintain a parcel against gravity with that of a developmentally retarded child. The child with a well-developed knowledge of the centre will stay curled up, even if only for a few moments.

Forward and backward somersaults (see Chapter 1) teach the child to stay curled up while upside down, and to keep curled up throughout the activity. Sometimes a child will perform an arched back bend when attempting a somersault over a supporter's shoulder, instead of curling up and doing a forward roll. The child will need help in maintaining a

34 'Parcels'. This profoundly deaf child has good awareness of her centre

curled-up position, as it is not good for the spine to be extended so far back.

Besides teaching the child to curl up, somersaults also teach the child to transfer weight successively through the shoulders, back and hips. An 'educated trunk' indicates that the child can move with free flow, flexibility and a high degree of body knowledge, and awareness of how to transfer weight through the body in an economic and fluent way.

Rotation in the trunk

Curling up is a symmetric movement, but twisting is asymmetric and is seen when one part of the body initiates a turning movement, followed by another part of the body. This is seen most clearly when the child is lying on the floor and rolls sideways in a flexible, sequential way, with the shoulders leading the roll followed by the hips, or vice versa. Many children roll in a rigid way, like a log, and will need help to obtain a twist in the trunk. The aim of the flexible roll is to develop flexibility in the body, mobility in the joints of the spine, and fluency in movement.

Rotation in the trunk is also experienced when the child moves from one activity to another, making smooth transitions between the activities. For example, children might sit on the floor, spin on their bottoms, fall over sideways, roll onto their stomachs, and then with a quick twist, sit up again. This involves preparing the body for each new position and action in a sequential way, and demands intelligent use of the body in the management of weight.

An energetic rotation is experienced when children lie on their stomachs with no limbs touching the floor. With a quick twist they roll onto their back, again with only the back touching the floor. Face down, the body is in an open position; on the back the body is in a closed position. A series of rolls and twists in this fashion develops a flexible, mobile use of the trunk, and is enjoyed by more able children.

Learning how to fall

It is important for all children to learn to fall safely and without hurting themselves, but this is even more important for children with learning difficulties. Children can learn in progressive stages how to fall.

1 The smallest fall of the body is experienced when the body lies on one side and falls onto the back (see page 10).
2 The next fall is experienced from a sitting position on the floor with the knees bent and wide apart in a cross-legged position. The body falls to one side, weight is transferred to the thigh, onto one hip, onto the elbow, upper arm and shoulder, and then onto the back, the body remaining in a ball shape throughout. The knee, thigh, hip, arm, shoulder and back can melt quite softly into the ground. The body can then swing up onto the other side so that the child rises up into a sitting position again. The body is experienced as a rolling ball.
3 Children can curl up, face down on the floor, roll sideways onto their back and continue the roll until they are face down again. This curled-up roll is helped if the children slide their knees apart, which makes

35 A middle school boy prepares for a four-point landing and a sideways roll

the transition of weight smoother and more fluent. The children also push with hands on the floor.

4 The next stage is to fall from a position on all fours. The child sinks to one side onto the floor, preparing the trunk to take weight by bending one arm so that the elbow, upper arm and shoulder are ready to support the body. At the same time the knee, thigh and hip of the same side rest on the floor until the child rolls smoothly onto the back. The roll can be continued until the child is on all fours again. This sideways fall and roll is the most comfortable way of falling. It can be practised on a mat, and it is a useful landing strategy when jumping and landing from a height. The body has to turn sideways in the air before the landing. The child lands on hands and feet – a four-point landing – as if he or she was pouncing on the floor; the child then tumbles sideways and rolls.

5 The child can be helped to fall from a kneeling position and then from a standing position. Each time the body 'melts' on one side and parts of the body are ready to take weight safely and fluently.

6 The next stage is to jump on the spot and land on the feet and hands in a pouncing action, and then let the body dissolve into a sideways roll as before.

7 The last stage is to run and jump, make a slight turn in the air so that the body can land with a pouncing action – a four-point landing – and then roll sideways in the same pathway as the run (Fig. 35).

Flying and falling call for extremes of weight management, and extremes of height and depth. More able children enjoy running and falling; some fall and slide, some fall and tumble. Less confident, less skilled children need plenty of experience in the earlier stages of learning to fall, so that they develop confidence in the mastery of their bodies. When they find that falling is not necessarily painful, they are more prepared to tackle gymnastic apparatus which involves leaving the ground. In preparation for gymnastics it is helpful to teach falling onto crash mats. These give children with severe learning difficulties encouragement to jump from a height. The aim of all movement education is to develop self-confidence in children through increased body mastery and control.

Part Two | *WHY WE TEACH IT*

Movement analysis: The diagram above has been adapted from Laban's movement theory as follows.

The circle in the centre of the diagram represents the whole body, both the central part and the extremities. Below this are the two opposite attitudes to gravity: giving in to gravity (allowing it to work on the body), and going against gravity. The six directions in space are listed on the left. Above the circle are relationships with others, and on the right are the movement qualities; the arrows within the box indicate that they are on a continuum. The word 'gentle' is used here rather than 'light' (a more appropriate word might be 'sensitive'), and flow is described as 'controlled' rather than 'bound'. 'Quick' and 'slow' replace Laban's terms 'sudden' and 'sustained'.

3

Movement analysis: Laban movement theory

Laban developed his theories of movement during his lifetime, and by the time he came to England in 1938 most of his ideas had crystallised. I have taken aspects of his movement analysis that are relevant to the needs of the people I teach and have developed a diagram which encapsulates these aspects of human movement (see below). Teachers of movement benefit from personal experience of these different aspects of movement; they need to be aware of *what parts* of the body are moving, in *which directions* in space they are moving and, most important, *how* the body is moving.

Laban's movement analysis falls into three main parts.

MOVEMENT ANALYSIS

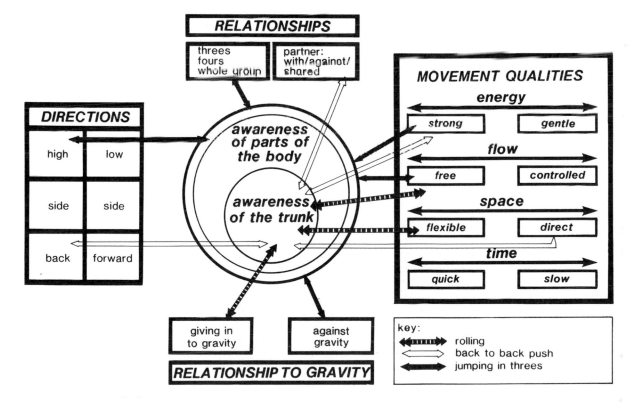

1   What part of the body is moving?

In order to assess this, the observer should ask him- or herself the following questions:

- Is the body moving as a whole, or is only one part of the body moving?
- Is the top half of the body involved in the movement, or is it mainly the lower part of the body that is moving?
- Is the central part of the body moving, or is movement confined to the periphery (hands and feet)?
- Are the 'halfway points' – the elbows and/or the knees – being used?
- Is the body moving in a coordinated way?

The body may move in different ways:

(a) in a *successive* way, as for example in hitting or throwing – the different parts of the body move sequentially;
(b) *simultaneously*, for example in a thrusting or pressing action – in a pushing action against a partner the whole body should move in one direction at the same time.

2   In which directions in space is the body moving?

Laban describes the movement of the body in six directions: backwards/forwards, high/low, side to side. Teachers can encourage children to move in directions that are normally neglected and thus enrich their awareness of space.

Backwards and forwards   On the whole, everyone moves naturally forwards, and the teacher will have to suggest to the children that they can move backwards, or extend a limb backwards. Using space behind them is difficult for children with severe learning difficulties, because they cannot see what they are doing.

High and low   Extending high into space and moving low at ground level should involve the whole body. Often an arm reaches high while the head continues to look forwards, and there is no upward intention in the trunk. Movement low down, at ground level, is often avoided. The greatest extension in these directions is the experience of a leap followed by a fall, first defeating gravity, and then giving in to it. This activity is much enjoyed by primary school children who have been taught how to land correctly (see Chapter 2). When the body moves upwards, this is often accompanied by a feeling of lightness, weightlessness, and when the direction of the movement is downwards, as in a pressing action, the movement is often accompanied by strength.

Sideways   Movement sideways is a further help in awareness of spatial directions. If both arms move symmetrically sideways, the body inevitably opens out. If the arms come close to the body, cross the mid-line and move towards the opposite side, the body moves into a closed position. The legs can also move far apart sideways, or cross over in a scissor-like action. The whole body can move sideways. When working on awareness of knees, the teacher can suggest that the children move their knees backwards, sideways, high and low, and encourage them to develop their own ways of exploring space (see Chapter 2).

These six directions constitute what Laban called the *Dimensional Scale*. He developed far more complex scales in the three-dimensional use of space, and he emphasised the importance of the pathways of movement connecting points in space.

If children have not developed awareness of their bodies, movement into space becomes meaningless and empty. With the development of some body awareness, the spatial directions begin to have greater significance.

Words such as 'behind', 'backwards', 'in front', 'sideways', 'beside', 'high', 'low', 'on top', 'under', 'over', have meaning for the child because they have been physically experienced by the body.

3 How, and in what way, is the body moving?

This is the most important of Laban's movement analysis, and the most difficult to describe. To be understood, this aspect of movement needs to be fully experienced. Laban separated out four distinct aspects of human movement:

- An attitude to *energy* (also referred to as *weight* or *force*)
- An attitude to the *flow* of movement
- An attitude to the *spatial pathways* of movement (which is different from directional movement in space; movement may involve all three dimensions)
- An attitude to *time*

He called these aspects of movement *motion factors*, or *movement elements*, and defined them as *energy, flow, space* and *time*, respectively.

He described the opposite attitudes to these motion factors either as 'fighting against them' or as 'indulging in them' (or enjoying them).

Energy Contrasting attitudes to energy can be expressed, at one end of the spectrum, as 'extreme strength', and at the other end as 'extreme lightness' or 'fine touch'. There are many gradations in between.

Flow This may be a difficult concept to appreciate. The person who fights against the flow of movement is very controlled and can arrest the movement at any time. The movement is under the control of the will. The opposite attitude to the flow of movement is seen when the movement is out of control; once started it cannot easily be stopped. This is seen, for example, in hitting and throwing actions, in spinning and turning movements, in rolling, jumping and running. Some dance styles accentuate controlled or bound flow, as in the pavane and minuet. The whirling dervishes, for example, demonstrate continuous free flow. Exaggerated free flow can produce a trance-like state.

Laban also described another aspect of flow – broken flow – where movement is jerky and arhythmic.

Space   There are two opposite attitudes to space. A person who fights space moves along straight lines, using space economically. The result is direct, linear movement. Direct intention and direct movement are well illustrated, for example, in the actions involved in playing snooker. On the other hand a person who enjoys space moves three-dimensionally, using all the space available: behind, in front, above, below, at each side. The pathways in space are curved, flexible, twisting, convoluted. Flexible winding-up and unwinding movements of the body are seen in a tennis service, although the flight of the ball is directed. There are many degrees in the use of space involving one-dimensional, two-dimensional and three-dimensional movements.

Time   This is a relatively easy motion factor to observe. Some people move quickly, suddenly, hastily, and fight time; others indulge in time and move slowly and with sustainment. In school and in daily living, emphasis is for the most part on speed. It is rare to see a truly sustained movement. It can be seen in the Noh theatre of Japan, and in some yoga movements where the emphasis is on the inner experience of the movement. Sudden movement is particularly dramatic when it follows stillness or slow movement.

Movement qualities   We now have eight movement qualities:

1	strong	3	bound flow	5	direct	7	fast
2	light	4	free flow	6	flexible	8	slow

On the whole, in teaching or observing young children, we are mainly aware of one or perhaps two of these qualities. It is rare to see as many as four at once.

If we take all the fighting attitudes – strength, bound flow, directness and suddenness – we get a punch or a thrust. The opposite attitudes – lightness, free flow, flexibility and sustainment – produce a floating action. *Punch* and *float* are two of Laban's eight *efforts*, which are the different combinations of the eight qualities of movement. Some people use *gliding* movement, involving light, bound flow, direct and sustained qualities. Others use *hitting* actions, involving strength, free flow, flexible and quick qualities. The four other efforts are *press*, *wring*, *flick* and *dab*.

As teachers we should concentrate on the eight movement *qualities* listed above, noticing which are present, which are latent, and which are absent, because this influences what we teach.

In the diagram on page 55, three activities – rolling, the back-to-back push, and jumping in threes – are represented by different arrows. These arrows indicate the different aspects of movement which are taking place at the same time. In a simple action such as rolling on the floor or on a mat, it is mainly the trunk that is involved. Children should move flexibly and with free flow, allowing gravity to help. Some children will roll in a rigid way with controlled flow and no flexibility; these children must be encouraged to roll in a more relaxed way.

In an activity such as back-to-back pushing, it is mainly the back that is involved, although the 'sticking power' comes from the hands and feet. The attitude towards energy is one of strength, the direction is backwards, the flow is controlled, and there is an 'against' relationship to a partner.

The arrows in the diagram that relate to jumping in threes, with two people pushing the one in the middle as high as possible (see Fig. 19), describe the main thrust of the group, although they are not all doing the same action. The whole body is involved, the movement is strong in an upward direction, and the movement is on a direct pathway.

The teacher of movement must be aware of which *parts* (or part) of the body are mainly involved in an activity, which *quality* of movement needs to be established, and in which *direction* the person is moving. The children learn about themselves through partner work. The teacher can then introduce work in threes, fours or fives, and eventually in larger groups.

Laban's movement analysis provides the structure that the teacher needs to understand in order to know what to look for in human movement. As a result of this observation, the teacher can decide what to teach.

4

Observation of Movement

The ability to observe and analyse human movement is the most important skill needed for movement teaching. The most significant aspect of movement that we need to observe is *how* children move.

What to assess

The teacher or caregiver should assess the following:

1 *Children's strengths*   The adult establishes those ways of moving which come most easily and naturally to a particular group of children. Their movement experiences must be successful. These different ways of moving, or qualities of movement, vary from one group to another and from one child to another. Each movement session should be appropriate for that group.

2 *Latent movement qualities*   These are ways of moving which children need to develop in order to acquire a more varied movement vocabulary. It is possible to change one aspect of a motion factor: for example, children who always tend to move quickly can be encouraged to move more carefully and slowly; children who appear to have no energy can be helped to discover a little strength.

3 *Movement qualities which are absent*   In some children who are disturbed, the movement pattern is lopsided: some qualities are exaggerated while the opposite ways of moving are not expressed.

Aims

The aim of movement observation is to help children to develop an all-round, balanced movement experience so that they can move in an appropriate way according to the many different physical tasks which they are presented with. Children need to be extended in their range of movement qualities and to have as rich an experience in ways of moving as possible.

Most children demonstrate quite clear preferences for certain ways of moving, and these ways of moving reflect their whole personality. Some children may find it difficult to direct their energy and to focus attention;

others may find it difficult to move flexibly and with free flow. Some children may not be in touch with their energy and appear listless and apathetic; others may show exaggerated strength. Some children may move slowly with fine touch; others may move with marked bound flow and are very tense.

Laban's movement analysis helps the teacher or caregiver to observe in a non-judgemental way (see Chapter 3). Movement sessions can be both diagnostic and therapeutic. The adult decides which activities are beneficial for children and helps the children to achieve, as far as possible, a balanced repertoire of movement experiences.

Through careful observation of movement, the teacher or caregiver can read signals given by the children and assess when it is necessary to change from one activity to another. The adult may see that the children need a new stimulus, or are ready for an activity which is perhaps more controlled, or more sensitive. Each movement session is a journey through a variety of ways of moving which the children need to experience but would normally neglect.

The ability to observe movement develops with practice. Besides being able to observe children's movement patterns, teachers and caregivers also need to be aware of their own movement preferences and limitations, because these will have a marked effect on the children they work with. Ideally, adults need to experience the full range of movement qualities themselves. They can then decide which ways of moving come most naturally to them, and become aware of the movement qualities that they tend to neglect and are less likely to incorporate into their own teaching. In order to provide a balanced, all-round movement experience for children, adults need to develop as balanced a movement repertoire as possible.

Benefits to the teacher

Two examples are given of how movement observation can help the teacher.

The teacher worked with a group of boys who were emotionally and behaviourally disturbed. They were extremely energetic and enjoyed strong, quick activities. Their concentration span was short and the boys needed to be constantly challenged with new activities, though they derived little experience from them. They each had a social work student as a partner, and during their first movement session the boys tended to dominate and exploit the willingness of their partners. They enjoyed a sense of power over the adult. Gradually though, over six sessions, they came to see the adults in a more positive light and began to relate in a more caring and sensitive way. Activities became less competitive and group work and cooperative play developed. It is important to give children like these the rumbustious experiences they crave, and then, as it becomes possible, to lead them towards experiences which touch their more caring feelings, and which are calm and quiet. This may be achieved, to a greater or lesser degree at the end of a session when the children feel satisfied and exhausted. The adults probably feel exhausted as well, but are rewarded by getting to know a child in a non-verbal way and by the change in the child's mood from uncontrolled energy to one which is relaxed and peaceful.

The opposite situation was observed among a group of pre-school children partnered by nursery nurses. The children were happy to be safely contained and cradled and made no attempts to instigate a different activity. They were encouraged to take the initiative in different ways, for example by sitting on the adult's back while she lay prone on the floor, or by crawling under the adult when she was on all fours. These children had to be helped to find the confidence to play, to discover their energy and strength, and to initiate activities. This process took several weeks and was largely achieved by developing free flow.

Some children need to get closer to their feeling and sensitivity, others need to experience their power and strength.

Observing children

A class of children   Here the teacher has to 'read' the group. As a rule the children leave the confines of the classroom full of energy. The movement experience they crave is quick, energetic and free flowing, and the teacher can find many ways of employing this energy usefully. Most young children enjoy speed, strength and free flow, though these qualities may be more apparent in boys than in girls. The content of a movement lesson for children is discussed in Chapter 5. The teacher should base the lesson on what he or she perceives the children need to experience, and should assess the different ways in which the children can extend their movement. This may involve increased body awareness and increased space awareness. Developing new ways of moving does not come so naturally to some children; for example, movement which demands sensitivity and gentleness, slowness, concentration, and the ability to 'listen' to what is going on in their own bodies. Children derive a sense of satisfaction from experiencing a variety of ways of moving, and the teacher should try to balance the opposites, although this may not be possible in the beginning.

Sometimes, rather than taking a lesson relevant to the needs of the majority of the class, a teacher may steer the activities towards the particular needs of one child. This child may be disruptive or extremely lacking in confidence.

The skilled observer of movement will be able to take movement ideas from different members of the class. This encourages the children to work hard because they realise that their efforts are being noticed, and also encourages the children to be inventive in developing the teacher's ideas. The greater part of a movement lesson can grow from what the children discover for themselves, as long as the teacher is quick to see innovative and educationally valuable ideas. The children gain a great deal from trying out each other's movements, and from learning from each other.   63

Babies   A baby's earliest movements can be described as 'global' – all its limbs move vigorously in a random way. Its legs kick strongly and quickly and, as the knee joint is a hinge joint, the action of kicking is direct. A baby's grasp of the adult's finger can be so strong that the adult, pulling the child by both hands, can raise the child a little way. This is best done when a baby has developed head control. Fine touch can also be seen in a baby's hand and finger movements, and a baby will pass a toy ring carefully from one hand to another. Carefulness involves bound flow and sustainment as well as fine touch. These fine touch and careful movements are accompanied by a direct and focusing gaze. The child demonstrates directness especially with the eyes, and every encouragement to direct attention should be given. Reaching movements are at first uncontrolled, but gradually the baby learns to make direct movements in attempts to grasp objects.

A baby shows flexibility when he or she attempts to roll over. As one part initiates the turn, the rest follows. A baby's body is also flexible when he or she squirms in pain; this squirming is a mixture of flexibility and strength, producing counter tensions in the body. When placed face down a baby will demonstrate strength by lifting the head and will eventually push against the supporting surface. Strength is seen in all movements against gravity.

Body awareness is seen when the baby plays with the feet and hands. The adult can feed in bodily sensations by tickling, patting, stroking and rubbing the baby's body. Initially the baby is only able to relate to those parts of the body that are easily seen.

Young children   As already stated, most young children enjoy quick, lively, energetic movement. They enjoy repetition of movements and many respond to music and enjoy rhythmical movement. They move spontaneously and rarely show signs of exhaustion or tiredness. When young children work with adolescents or adults they enliven the proceedings with their energy and enthusiasm.

Young children respond well to the challenge of gaining body mastery, whether it is body awareness or developing skills on large fixed apparatus or small apparatus. The movements which they find difficult are those which require fine touch, sustainment, and controlled flow, and those which are restricted in size. Reading, writing and mathematics require close concentration and movements of hand and eye on a small scale, which do not come easily to the young child. These skills may be tackled more willingly if the child has first had the opportunity to express his or her abundant energy.

Older children   Older children, while still retaining their energy, are more able to control their movement and can develop a rich repertoire of ways of moving. Children aged between nine and eleven are perhaps at their most able and they can develop a high standard of body mastery, a wide range of movement qualities and can work well with each other. They are capable of many skills and agilities and they are physically confident. One should aim to help children retain this ability, and confidence should be encouraged during adolescence; sadly, it is often lost.

Children with severe learning difficulties

It is impossible to generalise about the movements of children with severe learning difficulties. However, it is possible to say that on the whole they do not display the opposites of strength and sensitivity or fine touch. They move in a middle register of movements which are neither strong nor gentle. Their movement generally is in the middle range, neither free flow nor controlled, neither flexible nor direct, neither quick nor sustained. Progress is made when these children develop some degree of body awareness and when they acquire some strength and gentleness, often against or with a partner. They will also risk a little free-flowing movement, and may acquire some ability to control movement. Concentration requires strength, direct attention and controlled flow, and these qualities can be developed. These children can also acquire a degree of flexibility in the body and an awareness of space around them. On the whole progress is slow but rewarding.

Down's Syndrome children

Children with Down's Syndrome vary but when they are young they have marked free flow and great flexibility of movement. In fact both these qualities of movements are often better developed in Down's Syndrome children than in children in mainstream schools. Some Down's Syndrome children develop a good degree of body awareness, and with good teaching many can take part in movement lessons along with mainstream children. Some of these children may become stubborn and dominating, but others are able to use strength in a positive way. Their difficulty may lie in fine motor control and focused attention. Socially the Down's Syndrome child is likely to be responsive in relating and taking care of other children. On the whole they are a joy to teach and usually have good feeling which is reflected in their well-developed free flow, flexibility and sensitivity to other people.

Hyperactive children

The main characteristics of a child who is hyperactive are exaggerated speed, free flow, and strength. The energy that such a child expresses is extremely disturbing to other people and is exhausting to deal with. The child does not concentrate or direct movement, but may be observant in a fleeting way. A hyperactive child shows no interest in his or her own body and avoids relationships. Many of these children like to be as high up as possible and will climb to dangerous heights; they avoid being grounded.

It is possible to form a relationship with a hyperactive child; strategies for doing this are discussed in Chapter 7.

Children with autistic tendencies

The main characteristics of movement in a child with autistic tendencies are bound flow, sustainment, and fine touch. These movement qualities are often accompanied by long periods of directed attention. Such a child is often obsessed by one particular object. He or she shows no interest in developing body awareness and avoids making relationships, but it is possible to get through to such a child in a one-to-one relationship. Ways of helping the child with autistic tendencies are discussed in Chapter 7.

Emotionally and behaviourally disturbed children

Again there is a great variety among children in schools for the emotionally and behaviourally disturbed. They mostly show extremes of movement qualities: one child will have enormous strength, and another no strength at all; one child will move hastily, and another will hardly move at all; one will demonstrate exaggerated free flow, and another will move with very bound flow. Most of these children show no interest in developing awareness of their own bodies and many find it extremely difficult to relate to another person.

These children respond to movement teaching if they have a good relationship with a member of staff, or if they are in a one-to-one situation with helpful adults, or even with older children. The emotionally damaged child is often intelligent, living in a world where he or she can trust no one, but if the child finds it possible to trust another person, that child has the potential for development. An aggressive child can show his or her tender side as a result of movement experiences in relationship play, and a withdrawn child can begin to relate and respond to other people. Whereas the development in children with severe learning difficulties is slow, the development of emotionally or behaviourally disturbed children can be sudden, dramatic and very rewarding.

The questionnaire on pages 67–8 was originally intended for teachers of children with severe learning difficulties, but it can be adapted according to the needs of other children.

Child's Name .... Age ....

Approximate level at which child functions ....

....

Observation of relationship between child and partner

1. Can child let partner take his or her weight?   Partially ☐   Fully ☐

    In which activities?...

    ....

2. Can child make eye contact?   Yes ☐ No ☐

    When did this occur?. ....

3. Does child like being contained?   With free flow ☐   With support ☐

4. Can child take care of partner?   Yes ☐ No ☐

    In what ways does child take initiative?...

    ....

5. Can child balance with partner (mutual trust and support)? Yes ☐ No ☐

6. Can child understand what partner says?   Yes ☐ No ☐

    Does child respond to voice sounds?   Yes ☐ No ☐

7. Can child speak?   Yes ☐ No ☐

    What words are used? ....

    ....

Observation of child's self-awareness

Whole body

8. Can child trust own weight on the floor?   Partially ☐   Fully ☐

    In which activities? ....

9. Does child enjoy free-flow movement?   Yes ☐ No ☐

    In what form? ....

67

10. Can child be firm and stable?　　　　Yes ☐ No ☐

    In what ways? ....

11. Can child direct and control strength?　Yes ☐ No ☐

    In which activities? ....

12. Is the child aware of his or her middle?　Yes ☐ No ☐

    Can child curl up?　　　　　　　　Yes ☐ No ☐

Parts of the body

13. Is the child aware of knees?

    In sitting　(no weight)　☐　　In standing (weight-bearing)　☐

14. Is child aware of other parts of the body?

    Feet ☐　　　Hips ☐　　　Hands ☐　　　Elbows ☐

    Face ☐　　　Back ☐　　　Stomach ☐

General Observations

15. Can child relate to another child?　Yes ☐ No ☐

    To two or more?　　　　　　　　Yes ☐ No ☐

    How? ....

    When? ....

16. When did partner and child make the best contact? ....

    ....

17. When was child most involved? ....

    When did child concentrate best? ....

18. How did trust and confidence develop? ....

    ....

68 ....

Part Three | HOW WE TEACH IT

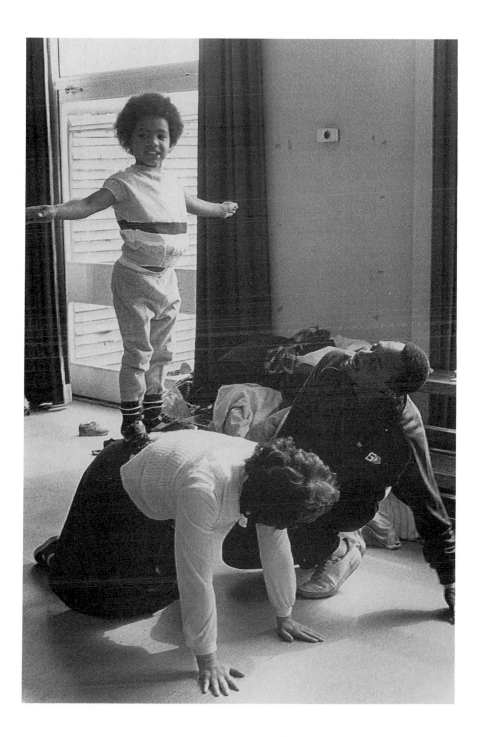

5

Content, structure and methods of teaching

Children with severe learning difficulties

The introductory session

Children with severe learning difficulties are usually in quite small classes, perhaps of six to ten children. These small numbers are necessary because the class will include children with a very wide range of abilities and disabilities. If you are a teacher working with a class of children for the first time, it is important to establish the group, and to help the children to relate to you. First of all, it is important to learn each child's name; to help with this, and to give the children a sense of security, ask the class teacher to join the group. Call the children to come and sit down close to you so that everyone is in a close physical group. To learn each child's name, put your hand on the shoulder or knee of each child, one at a time, and make eye contact. Tell the children your name, having first established if the school uses surnames or first names. This introduction is significant because the children have time to get to know you, and they enjoy seeing if you can remember their names.

If the group is shy and intimidated by the situation, you can gather the children together at one end of the room, sitting on a mat. In order to establish the group further, ask them all to move backwards on their bottoms with you, then all move back into the group again, close to each other. Moving on bottoms is done by pushing on the floor with the hands and feet. Do not ask the children to sit in a circle, but note which children sit on the outside of the group. Repeat this several times, moving backwards away from each other and towards each other, making it more interesting by moving into the group more quickly than when moving away. This emphasises the meeting of everyone together.

After a final movement away from each other, lie on your stomach and ask all the children to do the same. There is now more room between the members of the group, who are probably almost in a circle. Again move forwards towards each other, pulling with hands and elbows on the floor, then push with hands and move backwards away from each other. Eye contact between the children and the teacher or teachers is encouraged by the floor level, which limits the eye's range of vision. Some of the best eye contact is made along the floor. Everyone can lie on the floor and smack the floor loudly with the hands, a kind of drumming which the children enjoy.

When the children have moved backwards and the class has opened out, sit up and ask them to sit up as well, then spin round on your bottom and ask the children to try this. Push hard with the hands and ask them to do the same. Someone always falls over – this should be taken up as something for everyone to try, so that the activity becomes one of spinning, falling and sitting up again. Choose a child with a particularly skilful tumble and ask that child to demonstrate, and then ask everyone else to try to do the same. Gradually the group expands as children realise they need more space for this activity. It is important not to ask the group to spread out; they will make the decision to find a suitable space for themselves when they are ready.

The next development is to ask the children if they can roll. You may need to demonstrate this for a less confident class. Again, you can ask a child who rolls easily to show the rest of the children. All the time these activities are going on, call out and praise individual children by name and encourage everyone for the slightest effort. If one child sits and watches and does not join in, do not worrry about it. The child is usually noticing everything that is going on and he or she may join in eventually.

Usually these activities are novel to the children. They join in because the teacher participates in the activity, and encourages and is interested in the individual members of the group.

According to the response of the class and to their ability, you can go on to develop the introductory lesson in different ways. You can call them all together and say, 'Shall we run round the room?'. If the group looks eager to do this, everyone sets off round the room; some will run freely, and some, for example those who are physically handicapped, will do their best.

Progressions   In the sequence of events described above we move from restricted movement to much freer movement; from rather bound-flow movement to the free flow of spinning and rolling; and from movement at ground level to moving away from the ground in standing and running.

Security   This sequence of activities begins with the security of the group and the security of the floor. The children also develop some security in their relationship with the teacher, and the fact that he or she uses their names plays a key part in this. The fourth type of security – security from the centre of the body – is helped by the falling and rolling activities, when the children feel their backs and stomachs against the floor.

The lesson

If a teacher knows a class well, a good place to begin is to have the children sitting in a circle with their legs stretched out in front of them. The teacher sits with them. The children begin by patting their knees, then bend and stretch their knees while holding them. The teacher accompanies this with the voice and when the knees are pushed straight, everyone can make a sound such as 'whoosh'; the movement should be quick.

SUGGESTED PLAN FOR A LESSON

1	Establishment of the group (children, teacher, teacher's aide). Emphasis on coming together.
2	Enlargement of group. Relationship maintained over a larger area.
3	Movement becomes more individual. Weight management in spinning, falling and sitting up. Development of capacity to make sequential movements. Variety of ways of doing this encouraged.
4	Rolling. Free flow of weight (contrast with rolling stiffly if necessary). Variety encouraged.
5	Away from the floor: running and jumping. Use of space increased.
6	Lesson develops to encourage self-awareness. Possible developments according to needs of class. * If children unaware of knees, spend short time on knee awareness. Repeat running involving use of knees. * Running, falling down and rolling. Sequential movement experience. * Jumping (What helps child to jump? Elbows, knees.) * Return to floor, spin on stomach. Creep along floor. Slide along floor on the back, using feet to push with.
7	End with *either* partner work: * rolling partner, or * sliding partner, or * cradling partner *or* group work: * whole class rolls or slides the teacher (if class is small)

The teacher can then go through some of the activities described in Chapter 2, working on awareness of knees without bearing weight, then move on to activities which are freer and for which the children will be ready, for example skipping or galloping round the room with high knees (see Fig. 33). After this, the teacher can again 'anchor' the children and introduce activities at floor level which help the children to manage the weight of the body in falling and rolling activities. In early lessons, the teacher will have to call the children together to show them the activity so that it is clear what he or she wants them to try. Later, when a good relationship has been established, the children will understand what is wanted and the demonstration will not be necessary. However, children always enjoy activities more if the adult joins in. Teachers become skilled at initiating a new activity by joining in and observing carefully any variations that children may develop, by accident, which it would be helpful for all the children to try.

Teachers of children with severe learning difficulties have to participate more in their movement lessons than teachers in mainstream schools because mainstream children understand language better and move with greater mastery and confidence. Teachers who participate in movement classes make good contact with their children; indeed, many teachers of children with severe learning difficulties say that they get to know their children better in movement classes than in any other lessons.

The teacher may feel that the children need to experience the freedom of running round the hall or gymnasium at the start of the lesson, coming to ground-based work at a later stage. The teacher should always remember though that children learn more about their bodies against the floor than when they are standing.

Whatever stage the teacher has reached with the children, the second part of the lesson should, if possible, involve partner work. Here the teacher may demonstrate rolling a child, showing the children how to look after their partners as they roll them, and also pointing out how relaxed the child is who is being rolled. The teacher may lie down and ask two or three children to roll him or her. The children can be arranged in partners, and anyone who finds relating very difficult can be partnered by the teacher or the aide, if there is one.

The teacher may decide to introduce sliding a partner (see Fig. 8) and can show the children how to do this. If the class involves older children helping younger children, then the older children will have been shown how to do this in their own movement classes. If the teacher is working on his or her own, the children can all give the teacher a slide. In this case the teacher provides a focus of attention for the children.

Children with severe learning difficulties enjoy sitting back to back, one partner pushing the other along the floor. See-saws are another easy partner activity (see Fig. 23), or one child can make an arch through which the partner creeps or crawls (as in Fig. 11). The basic plan for movement lessons with these children is to begin with self-awareness and then to move onto awareness of a partner. Partner work may develop so that three or four children work together, or even as a group.

It is possible to combine classes of children where there is only one or two years' difference in ages. In this case the two teachers share the lesson, perhaps with the help of their aides. The children enjoy the stimulus of other children to work with, but during the lesson the teacher may give each child a somersault over the shoulder, maintaining the teacher-child relationship. Lessons can end with a caring relationship of one child cradling another (see Fig. 2).

Primary or secondary school children can be brought in perhaps once a week to work with a child each. The whole lesson is concerned with development through relationship play (see Figs. 36 and 37, and pages 5–36).

Ideally there should be some form of physical activity every day for children with severe learning difficulties. This could be swimming, work on large fixed apparatus, work with small apparatus, movement, riding, outdoor pursuits or possibly dance and drama. Some teachers at the beginning may find it difficult to sustain a movement session for half an hour and could begin by teaching some activities which encourage body awareness and body mastery, then move on to work on or with apparatus, or even have a session on drama.

In the beginning it is difficult for children with severe learning difficulties to concentrate on their own bodies because they are more familiar with activities in relation to objects. This means that their attention span may be short and their interest hard to maintain, and the teacher may feel at a loss. However, if the teacher is convinced of the value of what he or she is doing, and is enthusiastic, the children will gradually learn to relate to their own bodies and to others, and their attention span will increase.

The development of body mastery and the capacity to relate to other people will help these children in all the other aspects of physical education in which they take part. It is best if they change into shorts and tee-shirts for physical activities. This gives them practice in dressing and undressing, and it helps them to move more freely. Children and visitors should be encouraged to work in bare feet if possible, as this helps the feet to develop greater sensitivity.

Children with moderate learning difficulties

Children with severe learning difficulties do not understand that they are in a special school and are not aware of having failed to enter a mainstream school. Children with moderate learning difficulties are aware that they have failed, and they are likely to have many emotional and social problems. Physically, many of these children are capable of being as able as mainstream children, but they often have a very low sense of self-worth. One sign of this is that they may have difficulty in making eye contact.

The teacher has to assess in which activities the children will feel safe and successful. The class may have a great deal of energy, or they may be diffident and unwilling to move and commit themselves. The teacher needs to select appropriate activities for that particular group of children in order to promote body awareness.

75

36 A middle school girl working with a young child with severe learning difficulties

37 Middle school boys swing a boy with severe learning difficulties

Children with moderate learning difficulties can gain confidence and self-esteem by participating in physical activities, because they are more likely to be successful in practical activities than in intellectual ones. It is very important that these children are successful in developing what skill they have, and experience a sense of achievement. The teacher has to be aware that he or she is working with children who have been emotionally damaged and who have experienced failure.

One group of children with moderate learning difficulties partnered children with severe learning difficulties. The children with moderate learning difficulties had experienced failure in physical education lessons in their own school, but in the school for children with severe learning difficulties they were successful and felt important in movement classes with the younger children. Evidence of this is that they never missed their weekly sessions in the school for children with severe learning difficulties.

Movement classes were held early every morning in one school for children with moderate learning difficulties aged seven to eight. The lesson often lasted an hour because the children kept on reminding the teacher of activities they wanted to do which she had left out. The teacher found that afterwards the children settled down to work in the classroom in a much better frame of mind than when they went into the classroom first thing in the morning. On one occasion the mothers of some of the children came to join in the movement session, so there was one adult for each child. Two of the mothers later remarked on how much their children had gained as a result of their movement classes.

A teacher in one school for children with moderate learning difficulties was successful in involving an older class working as partners with much younger children. Figures 28 and 38 to 41 illustrate this sort of partner work. Elsewhere, youngsters from a mainstream secondary school partnered children with moderate learning difficulties, and in another school, children with moderate learning difficulties, some of them with very low self-esteem, successfully worked with younger children with severe learning difficulties. In spite of their obvious lack of self-confidence, they made a good effort to partner children who were younger and less able than themselves.

Children with moderate learning difficulties need to have some form of physical activity daily. They need to experience success in their efforts in order to develop some degree of self-confidence, they need encouragement to focus attention and concentrate, and they need help in relating to other people.

Mainstream children

Children in mainstream schools look forward to their session in the school hall, whatever form it takes. Unfortunately the hall is usually timetabled for each class only once a week, perhaps twice, and sometimes the class teacher may not take up this opportunity for the class to be physically active.

38   An older girl with moderate learning difficulties helps a younger child in her school

39   A mutual hug. An older boy partners a younger pupil in a school for children with moderate learning difficulties

40   A younger child tries to cradle an older girl in a school for children with moderate learning difficulties

41   Older and younger children meet in a school for children with moderate learning difficulties

The movement class may begin according to the children's needs, or if the teacher is not very confident, the opening activity might be one in which the teacher knows that he or she can control the children. For example, if the teacher is working with primary school children he or she can call them all together (Fig. 42), and go over the children's names. They can be asked what they can remember of the lesson of the previous week.

Running

The teacher could begin by teaching the children how to run. This requires the driving power of the legs with emphasis on the knees. It requires strong action of the elbows, and all four limbs move on a forward-backward plane. It is common to see some children swing their arms from side to side as they run, which does not contribute to the running action. The teacher can pick out different running styles from among the children – some with long strides, some very energetic, some with a marked direct intention – and ask the children to try out these methods. When the teacher says 'Stop', the children should stop as immediately as they can, taking three or four steps to slow down. The aim is to develop speed in running. The children should only be stopped in order to give them a fresh directive to improve their skill.

Falling

The next stage in development is to teach falling. For this the children work through the stages in falling described in Chapter 2, beginning with falling sideways from a position on all fours. They work up to falling from standing, and falling from a jump on the spot. The falls all end in a roll. They then return to running but the run finishes in a fall and a roll (see Fig. 35). Again, ideas can come from the children on how best to manage the weight of the body so that the fall is comfortable and painless.

Rolling

If the class has difficulty giving in to weight or letting go of weight, it is important to do more work on rolling, helping the children to experience the body giving in to the pull of gravity, before returning to running and falling. It can be explained to the children that they are learning how to look after themselves if they should fall.

Awareness of the centre

It is now possible to move on to a quieter activity, using, for example, awareness of the centre as the theme. The teacher can ask the children to spin on their stomachs, using their hands to propel them round, encouraging them to smack the floor as they go. They can then curl up face down, and move in a curled-up position with knees close to elbows and head tucked in. The teacher can move onto 'opening and shutting' animals and other forms of locomotion close to the floor. If, during the running, it is noticeable that the children are not aware of their knees sufficiently to achieve a good action in the legs, the teacher can move on to activities that 'feed in' experience of the knees, perhaps in standing, such as smacking them, holding on to them, and doing many of the activities described in Chapter 2.

Working with a partner

The next stage is partner work. Partners may have been arranged in the classroom beforehand. If any child has a particular difficulty in moving, an able, caring child can take responsibility for this child. If there is a child

42 A headteacher of an infant school works with the reception class

43 Middle school boys help each other to somersault

with a behaviour problem, the teacher can work with this child. Partner work may start with back-to-back rides, or with rolling a partner, or sliding a partner. If the class is new to partner work, the teacher can demonstrate the activity, or ask a few children to roll or slide the teacher. As the children become more skilled in partner work, they can move on to shared relationships and 'against' relationships (see Figs. 25, 31 and 43). The lesson can finish with containing and rocking a partner; by this time the children should be able to shut their eyes and relax. If possible, the teacher should give each child a somersault over the shoulder at the end of a lesson. In this activity the teacher contains and supports each child and each child has to trust the adult. The most nervous and least confident child in the class is usually the last in line for the somersault. This activity is a good way for the teacher to relate to every child in the class. Learning to curl up will help the children to stay curled up during the somersault.

Beginner teachers should take a lesson in which the children are 'earthed' or 'anchored', as they are more easily controlled when they are close to the floor. Activities include spinning on stomachs, spinning on bottoms, spinning and falling, spinning, falling and rolling. Different kinds of rolling may be developed: stiff as a log, curled up, successive and flexible rolling. Children can learn to fall with increase in difficulty of the fall. If the teacher feels confident enough, the children may be encouraged to move round the room more freely. The teacher needs to know and use names, to praise effort, and to have complete quiet when he or she is describing the next activity. To achieve this he or she may have to ask the children to sit down and listen. The teacher must also use the minimum of talking to obtain the maximum physical activity. The children should feel pleasantly tired at the end of a session and must have a sense of achievement

It is difficult for a student teacher to see individual versions of an activity which would be useful for all the children to try, especially when classes number over thirty. There is greater richness and variety in children's movement than in adults' movement, and with practice the teacher will be able to pick out individual contributions to the lesson. It is important not to ask the same children to show their movement ideas each time, as the teacher needs to recognise the efforts of children who have a low estimation of themselves, however small their contribution may be. All the teacher needs to say is, 'Well done, so-and-so', to let the child know that his or her efforts have been noticed and appreciated.

It is always a challenge to control a large class in an open space such as a school hall after the confines of a classroom, but movement lessons give the teacher a chance to see another aspect of the children and an opportunity to enjoy an activity with the children. For some parts of the lesson the teacher may sit on the floor, and this can be a shock for children who are used to an authoritarian standing figure teaching them. Children may try to take advantage of a new young teacher and exploit the situation if they can. The teacher has to be firm and exert authority while at the same time being encouraging and appreciative of effort.

Planning the programme

The movement lesson should be carefully planned and the activities written down as a reminder. An experienced teacher will be able to see if the activities planned are appropriate and will be able to adjust accordingly. A teacher who is skilled in movement observation can have a flexible approach to the plan and will develop activities which the children discover for themselves. The teacher in this case has to concentrate hard and think quickly in selecting the most valuable variations on the basic theme. One of the most difficult decisions to make is how long a particular activity can be sustained and how long interest can be maintained. The activity is only beneficial so long as the children are obtaining a valuable experience as a result of it. Initially children do not sustain interest for very long but with practice their concentration span increases. An indication of a good lesson is how thoroughly a few activities have been explored. When a teacher starts this kind of work, he or she tends to cover a lot of ground superficially. This is because the children do exactly what the teacher asks and then stop, waiting for the next directive. Confident, inventive and energetic children will explore possibilities and will often, spontaneously, produce a lively activity which the teacher has not anticipated but which adds to the repertoire of the class.

The teacher also needs to be able to 'read' the class and see when an appropriate type of activity is needed, balancing energetic with more careful movement, free flow with controlled flow, strength with gentle movement, fast with slower movement. The teacher should, through observation, anticipate the children's physical need for an opposite type of activity before the children are even aware of this, so that the class does not become restless or perhaps over-excited. This restlessness or excitability is often evidenced by one child who acts as a kind of thermometer for the class. An observant teacher should not meet problems of children becoming bored or uninvolved or out of control, and all movement classes should be successful in fulfilling the needs of the children.

When teaching a class for the first time, the teacher will have to work in a firmer and more structured way than the teacher who has had time to forge a good relationship with the children and can teach in a more flexible way. The teacher's decision to give the children greater freedom in which to be inventive and show initiative will depend on his or her confidence and ability.

It is advisable to explain to the children why you are teaching certain activities. Even five- and six-year-old children can listen and benefit from the information.

There are some movement teachers who, while very effective, do not develop their classes from what they observe their children have discovered. Instead they feel secure with a prepared list of activities which they repeat from week to week. Gradually new activities are introduced as the teacher feels ready to try something new, and a repertoire of activities is developed. Each teacher has to choose a method of teaching with which he or she feels confident, and some teachers may find that a carefully structured series of activities gives them a sense of security. It is quite common for children to demand an activity which the teacher has forgotten to include in the lesson.

It is interesting at the end of a lesson to ask the children what they enjoyed most. 'Parcels' and 'prisons' seem to be particularly popular. Some of the children will say it is the activity at which they felt most successful, such as 'being strong'.

Teaching points

1 Do not have a 'front' from which to teach but move about among the children. Give the next directive from the back or side of the school hall, or from the centre. This also gives the teacher the opportunity to give a congratulatory pat on the shoulder to children who are doing well.
2 When the children run round the room, do not indicate which way they should run, but let them make the decision. Ask them, 'Which way shall we go?'. The majority run anti-clockwise, even in the first lesson.
3 Do not say when the children should start an activity such as 'Run' or 'Off you go'. It is better if the children make their own decision as to when to begin. It is very tempting to start off a class with a command, but if one is patient the children will soon realise it is up to them when to start. The teacher can say, 'Go when you are ready'.
4 The start and end of a movement class can be an essential part of the movement lesson. For example, one successful class began with several of the children, who had left their shoes in the classroom adjacent to the school hall, rolling into the room from the classroom door. Children with severe learning difficulties can travel back to their classroom in different ways, on their bottoms or sliding a partner. (This, of course, depends on the cleanliness of the corridors.)
5 On entering the hall, it is a good idea to ask the children to practise an activity from the previous week until everyone is ready. The teacher can then call the class together and ask them what they remember from the previous lesson.

Partner work When children work with a partner, the noise level goes up as the children talk to each other. The teacher should tolerate this as long as, at a signal, the children respond and are quiet. Such a signal might be clapping the hands, or calling out in low but carrying voice, 'Sit down everyone' or 'Stop everyone'. The teacher needs to use a low tone of voice; the same tone as the children only exacerbates the general noise level.

The teacher may be working with two classes, one older and one younger, and this will contribute to the noise level. The teacher who involves large numbers needs to have a high noise threshold and be able to control large numbers.

Group work It is a sign of progress when children can work well together in groups. One of the simplest developments of this arises from partner work when three couples join hands in a ring. They proceed to tie themselves into a knot without letting go of hands (Fig. 44). The knot is made by going under and over each other's arms. When firmly knotted the group can try to move, all in the same direction! They can sit down together, rise, and untie the knot without letting go.

Another group activity, originally suggested by a bright seven-year-old boy, is to make a tunnel through which children can creep (see Fig. 11). Several children on all fours might carry other children or the teacher in a long line on their backs (see Fig. 49). Four older children can give a fifth child a swing (Fig. 37). A 'pile' of people is enjoyed particularly by physically handicapped children.

Security   As has already been mentioned at the beginning of this chapter, there are four aspects of security: security with other people in the group; security with the teacher; security in connection with the floor; and security from the centre of the body, or having a 'home'.

While children growing into adolescence feel more secure with a partner than on their own, younger children do not find it easy at first to work with a partner, and this has to be regarded as something to aim for. However, if partner work is a regular experience for young children, this will give them confidence. One reception class which worked once a week with a junior class of nine- to ten-year-olds was able to partner a class of six-year-olds from a socially deprived area. They were immediately confident in partnering unknown older children from a multicultural school (see Figs. 9 and 45).

Relating movement to classroom work

Infants enjoy writing about and illustrating movement activities which they have done, particularly if partners from an older class are involved. It is interesting to check in their drawings of the human body whether the legs are depicted as a straight line, or if knees are drawn in and the line bent. An art teacher in a school for children with severe learning difficulties noticed that one girl introduced a trunk into her paintings of herself where before the legs had been attached to a round shape depicting the head and body combined. The teacher felt this was the result of her increasing awareness of having a centre to her body.

Many forms of locomotion along the floor can be likened to movements of animals, and one can devise a lesson on evolution, beginning with creatures with no limbs who can only wriggle, and then moving on to the development of limbs and the animals that can creep and crawl and hop and spring.

A project on 'myself' or 'me' can be connected with the development of body awareness. There are many action words which can be learnt arising from movement lessons, for example 'creeping', 'slithering', 'sliding', 'rolling', 'falling', 'opening', 'shutting'. Words are more meaningful if they are connected with a physical experience.

If movement is well taught in a school, it should have an effect on the way children conduct themselves in the classroom. If older children   85

44 Primary school boys work with reception children to make a 'knot'

45 A reception class child partners a boy from a multicultural school. Rolling a partner with the feet

46 A primary school child helps a reception class child to jump

47 A nine-year-old makes a 'tunnel' for four-year-old reception class children

partner younger children within a school, this will help both groups to relate to each other and will help the younger children to behave with some of the maturity of the older children (Figs. 46 and 47). Effects of good movement teaching may be seen at playtime as well as in more organised aspects of school life. An increase in self-esteem, a feeling of security with other children in the school, and the development of skills in building relationships, can have a positive effect on a whole school.

| *SPECIAL CHALLENGES*

6

Movement for children and adults with profound and multiple learning difficulties

On the whole it is teachers and physiotherapists who work with people with profound and multiple learning difficulties (PMLD), and they are faced with many difficult problems and challenges. The number of children with PMLD appears to be increasing, and there is a demand for methods which will help adults with PMLD in subnormality hospitals and in hostels. Movement for both adults and children has to be carried out on a one-to-one basis and, as the adults become heavier and more difficult to move, two people may be needed to work with one adult. Working with children and adults with PMLD can be physically stren-uous and is time-consuming. Methods of working with adults are included in this section because the movement experiences involved are similar for both children and adults.

Description

People with profound and multiple learning difficulties are severely physically handicapped and have severe learning difficulties. Some may function at the level of a child of a few months old. The older people in hospitals and hostels are often institutionalised and may have deterior-ated so that they are isolated and do not communicate. They may have developed self-mutilating behaviour or obsessive movements as a result of the lack of external stimuli.

The range of ability and disability of people with PMLD is very wide, so it is difficult to devise a programme which suits everyone; each person has individual needs. They may suffer from different kinds and degrees of spasticity or cerebral palsy. In this condition spasticity may occur in one or more limbs or may involve spasticity in the trunk and all four limbs. The flexor muscles are stronger than the extensors so that, for example, wrist and elbows become bent. Adductor muscles in the thighs are stronger than the abductors so that a scissor position results. Occasionally there is an extensor reflex when the handicapped person arches backwards. Some people with PMLD may be flaccid and have very little muscle tone, and others may have uncontrolled movement. Some people may have little or no voluntary movement except perhaps of the eyes. They may have no language and may not understand language, but will respond to the tone of voice of the caregiver. They may be partially sighted or have no sight at all, and they may be hearing impaired or profoundly deaf. They may avoid eye contact. They may not be able to sit or roll over. Some people may be able to sit up, some may possibly take weight in standing with support, and some may be able to walk with help. Life can be made more difficult for those who work with people with PMLD if one or two in the group are not physically handicapped and are mobile but have marked emotional and behavioural difficulties. These people may be destructive and aggressive to others in the group.

Aims

- To help the children or adults to form relationships as far as they are able
- To feed in physical sensations which promote body awareness and control and a sense of well-being
- To provide appropriate stimuli of all kinds to help children or adults develop their resources as far as they are able
- To encourage independence and initiative wherever possible
- To improve the quality of life for the profoundly handicapped

Social and emotional needs

Supporting and containing

Everyone needs to feel secure and needs to be able to relate to other people, though the ability of the profoundly handicapped to experience this may be very limited. The teacher, caregiver, parent or therapist can give a sense both of security and of confidence through activities such as supporting and containing. Supporting the weight of someone with PMLD, in whatever way, is significant, because in committing his or her weight the adult or child demonstrates confidence in the supporter and in himself or herself. Supporting can be partial or full.

Cradling

An example of supporting and containing is cradling; the caregiver sits behind the handicapped person, making his or her body into a 'chair', and gently rocks the person from side to side, accompanied by humming or singing. (See Fig. 48 and Chapter 1.) Children can also be rocked backwards and forwards to the point where the child is almost upside down. This is much enjoyed by children, and is also enjoyed by adolescents, but the supporting partner in this case has to be particularly strong. The free flow of the cradling helps to reduce spasticity, promotes a relationship between supporter and supported, and prepares the handicapped person for further movement experiences. Cradling can be used as a preparation for speech therapy.

Supporting

The caregiver can lie on his or her back and support the handicapped person full length along his or her front (see Fig. 6). The handicapped person lies face down with arms and legs spread out on each side of the

48 A senior boy in a school for children with severe learning difficulties supports and contains a girl who has profound and multiple learning difficulties

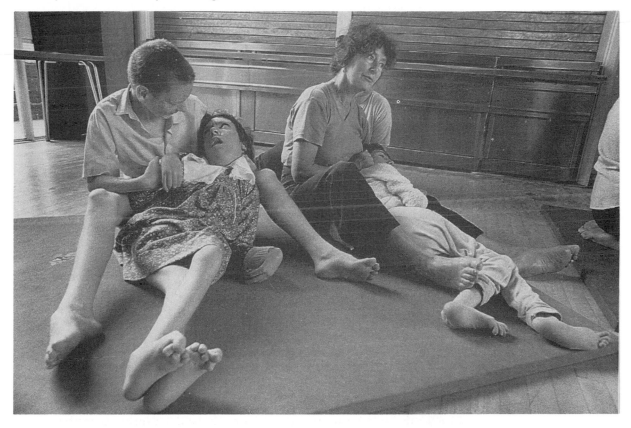

caregiver. This is probably the best position in which to achieve relaxation. The caregiver embraces the handicapped person and may sway gently from side to side. This is a good position for achieving eye contact, although the caregiver may be dribbled on.

The supporter can lie face down and the handicapped person is laid along the caregiver's back, also face down. Again the limbs are encouraged to fall to each side of the caregiver's body, unless the handicapped person has tense, spastic legs and arms. It is often difficult to open out an adult who has developed a curled-up, flexed position, but it can often be achieved by gentle means, and gradually the stiff, institutionalised adult lets go, even when this is a completely new experience. The caregiver can rock gently or hump his or her back gently. The aim of both these experiences is to encourage relaxation and to help the handicapped person feel his or her body against another human body and establish a primitive form of communication. It is possible in this situation to feel a great physical warmth. This exchange of warmth between bodies helps the handicapped person to relax. Sometimes the relaxation is better when the handicapped person lies on the caregiver's front, and sometimes on the back.

Handicapped people need to feel their bodies against the bodies of others. There are many activities which feed in to the handicapped person that he or she has a body; this can be experienced through contact with another person, or through lying on the floor or other supporting surface. Emphasis is on the whole body experience and on the trunk as the centre which connects the head to the extremities. Sensorily deprived people, such as those who suffer from rubella and have little or no sight or hearing, particularly need this kind of sensory stimulation and information.

Bouncing   Another way of giving support is for the caregiver to sit on the ground with legs stretched out in front. The handicapped person lies face down across the caregiver's thighs with the stomach resting on the thighs. The caregiver can bounce or rock the handicapped person gently and this has a comforting effect; the gentle bouncing and rocking can help people who scream continuously to become quiet. Pressure on the solar plexus in a rhythmic movement of this kind has a calming effect. In this position a handicapped person can be patted up and down the spine, a sensation which is enjoyed. Gentle bouncing was used by a teacher to help a severely spastic boy who was too rigid to sit, to slowly relax until he was in an inclined sitting position in which he could be fed. The teacher sat on a chair and held the boy across her lap lying on his back. This process took fifteen minutes before the midday meal.

As described in Chapter 1, the handicapped person can lie on his or her back on a mat while the caregiver, kneeling beside the handicapped person, pulls the person onto his or her side to rest the stomach against the caregiver's thighs. The caregiver pulls on the handicapped person's hip and shoulder and then lets the person fall back onto the mat. This fall, giving in to the pull of gravity, helps the handicapped person to relax. This experience of falling should be repeated a few times, emphasising the heaviness of the drop onto the back.

Horizontal rocking   The sensation of the free flow of weight can be increased by horizontal rocking in which the handicapped person is pulled up on one side towards the caregiver, allowed to fall back, and then pushed gently up on to the other side and again allowed to fall back. This experience can reduce tension in the neck and can have a relaxing effect on the whole body.

Rolling   It may be possible to encourage the handicapped person to initiate a rolling action. If a child is involved, the child lies on his or her back. The caregiver bends the child's right knee across the child's body, thus making it easier for the child to start to roll to the left. A roll can also be started by gently pulling the right arm across the body; the caregiver lies on the floor and makes eye contact at floor level. The child's head may have to be turned or the child may voluntarily turn the head in order to look at the caregiver, who uses words of encouragement.

Sliding   Sliding along the floor is an enjoyable free-flow experience and this can be done with the handicapped person lying on his or her back on a blanket (see Fig. 10). A child who is very thin can be slid on a sheepskin rug.

Swinging   Adults with PMLD who have neck control can be swung by four supporters each holding a limb, and they will enjoy the free-flow movement and attention of four people; some tense adults may let go of the tension in their limbs. Children who are flaccid and do not have muscular control, and those who are very spastic, can be swung in a blanket. The handicapped person can be carried on the backs of supporters who are on all fours, and gently swayed (Fig. 49).

See-saws   See-saws can be done in threes with the handicapped adult supported by a caregiver sitting behind, while another caregiver sits in front holding the handicapped person's hands. Between them they help the handicapped person to lean backwards and forwards. Eye contact may be achieved here and the action can be accompanied with a song. If the caregiver is working with a child, only one caregiver seated in front is usually necessary.

Enjoyment comes from the free flow of weight and is experienced through such activities as cradling, rolling, sliding, bouncing, swinging and rocking. Free-flow movement of the whole body produces a harmonious state and helps the person with PMLD to relax, to trust other people and to begin to communicate.

Stages in relationship play

At first the person with PMLD receives experiences passively. Then there may be some signs of a response so that the caregiver is made aware of which activities the handicapped person prefers and enjoys. The person with PMLD may indicate that he or she wants to repeat the activity.

Obsessional movements begin to disappear as the handicapped person finds the movement experiences interesting and involving. The handi-   95

49 Seniors in a school for children with severe learning difficulties support a girl who has profound and multiple learning difficulties, and sway her gently

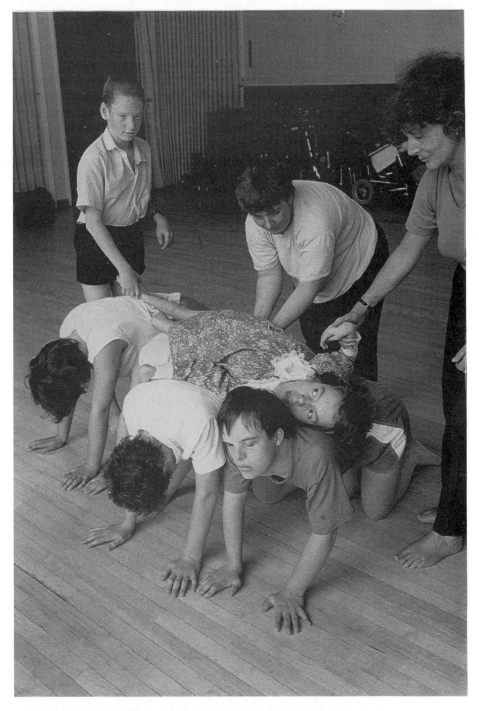

capped person starts to initiate activity and the caregiver should respond to these signals and make use of the activities to increase the handicapped person's repertoire of movement.

The handicapped person may be able to look after the caregiver in different ways, such as pulling the caregiver up in the see-saw movement, or cradling the caregiver or another handicapped person. This is important, as people with PMLD have little opportunity to look after someone else.

The role of the caregiver

Communication skills

The caregiver has to develop his or her communication skills in order to help handicapped people to cooperate and to extend their movement vocabulary and experiences. Eye contact and facial expression are important, as many people with PMLD respond to facial expression, voice and movement. The caregiver should whenever possible be at the same eye level as the handicapped person, and may sometimes be lower, giving the handicapped person an opportunity to look down at the caregiver.

Voice

Voice is particularly important as a means of communication, and voice sounds – humming, singing, and the use of descriptive words – all support the movement experiences. The voice should be kept low, quiet and encouraging, and it can also enhance the fun and enjoyment of the activities. The voice can be used rhythmically to accompany movement and the caregiver requires sensitivity in finding the right rhythm to suit each person. The voice therefore is a more appropriate accompaniment for activity than music; when music is used as an accompaniment to movement, the rhythm is imposed from an outside source and may not be appropriate. The handicapped person may make sounds during activities and the caregiver should respond to these either by imitating the sounds or giving a vocal response as though a conversation had developed. People with PMLD may even join in singing.

The caregiver starts with an activity which the handicapped person enjoys, develops variations on this, and gradually introduces activities which the handicapped person needs but would have initially rejected. The aim is to extend the range of movement experiences and to do this the caregiver may have to be firm but is also rewarding and encouraging. Some adults with PMLD may reject all human contact, and a few may be aggressive, and the caregiver may have a struggle to begin with. A calm approach and a sense of humour are very helpful, with the emphasis on play rather than on coercion. Sometimes the handicapped adult will observe that everyone else is enjoying themselves and will eventually consent to join in. Playing, and enjoying human contact, may be very strange for some adults. As the handicapped person finds the sensations enjoyable, and not threatening, resistance gradually decreases.

The caregiver has to be generous with his or her energy and the use of the body as a teaching resource. The shared experience is rewarding for both participants but is demanding for the caregiver, particularly when working with large adults with PMLD. A team of people working   97 together, partnering the handicapped in a movement session once a week, can make the job of building relationships and of feeding in necessary movement experiences more enjoyable and feasible.

Physical needs

While movement experiences can help to contribute towards the social and emotional needs of people with PMLD, their physical needs are also met by movement experiences, which help to reduce tension and promote some degree of self-awareness. Tension can be reduced by gentle stroking and by various free-flow experiences.

Some people with PMLD need to develop their strength, however limited this may be. Anti-gravity muscles need to be developed wherever possible. The significance of the development of back and neck muscles is described in Chapter 2. People with PMLD should be placed face down for some parts of the day, either in a lying position or supported by a wedge in a reclining diagonal position; this latter position allows the hands to be free, and both positions encourage symmetry of the body, which is very important for those people who have spasticity down one side of the body. There is a tendency for people with PMLD either to sit propped-up for long parts of the day, or to lie on their backs. Profoundly handicapped people will resist new positions, especially if they have spent many years lying on their back. Wherever possible, back muscles need strengthening in order to achieve a sitting position, and legs need to be strengthened in order to take weight in standing. A prone board inclined at an appropriate angle can help the handicapped person to stand in a stable position and develop some strength in the legs and, as in sitting, the hands are free to play with objects.

In order to help people with PMLD to get into a crawling position, a foam cylinder can be placed under the stomach and the person can be encouraged to take weight on hands and knees. The handicapped child, lying face down, can be pulled up into a crawling position by the caregiver, who stands astride above the child and who can adjust the support necessary for the child. If the child is small, the caregiver can support under the trunk with one hand while the other helps the limbs to move forwards in a crawling action.

Locomotion Profoundly handicapped people need encouragement to move independently, if this is at all possible. This may develop through rolling, creeping or crawling, eventually leading perhaps to standing and walking.

The physiotherapist is the best person to advise on suitable sitting and standing positions. Each person will need a different solution to his or her problems. The profoundly handicapped need to be manoeuvred gently into different positions during the day and should not be left in one position for a long time. The lifting and handling involved is best supervised initially by a physiotherapist.

Movement in water Water provides greater freedom of movement for profoundly handicapped people; they benefit from the increased range of movement, increased relaxation, and the stimulus that water can give. It is possible for some people with PMLD to move independently in water. Water is particularly helpful to those who suffer from rubella and who are profoundly handicapped both visually and aurally. People who are profoundly handicapped and whose bodies are asymmetric owing to spasticity on one side of the body, will have difficulty in balancing in water and some kind of inflatable support may be used. Each person with PMLD will need the support of a caregiver. For this, young people from secondary schools can partner the handicapped, under supervision.

On the whole it is necessary to have the water temperature several degrees higher for physically handicapped people. Hydrotherapy pools are warm and shallow, but in some places they are too small for more than a very few people.

Feeding and toileting
These ministrations take up a large part of the day for people with PMLD and it may be difficult to make time to give individual attention to everyone and to carry out the activities described. The same muscles are used in talking and eating. Some children have to be helped to masticate and gentle massage of the cheeks can be helpful. Cooperation with the speech therapist is also very helpful.

Planning a programme

It is a great help to people with PMLD if they can have a movement session once a week, when work can be done on a one-to-one basis. Ideally they also need a session in water at least once a week. Much movement work can be done in the classroom with individuals by the teacher and aides, with help from the physiotherapist. There is a tendency for profoundly handicapped children to stay in their classroom all day, but it is valuable fo them to be active in the school hall and have the stimulus of fresh people to work with. One way of providing a one-to-one working relationship is to enlist the cooperation of senior children with severe learning difficulties in the school, and to teach them how to carry out simple activities under supervision in movement sessions (see Figs. 6 and 10).

It is advisable to start a stimulating movement programme while children are young, to keep their bodies as mobile as possible and to teach them to accept and to make relationships. It is a very important contribution to the progress of children with PMLD if their parents can be involved in movement sessions, so that teachers, physiotherapists and parents can all work together for the benefit of the children. Carefully planned activities should be started as early as possible both at school and at home.

The situation is more difficult in hospitals and hostels for adults with PMLD, but where physiotherapists have initiated movement sessions involving a team of helpers, they have observed that the behaviour of these institutionalised adults has improved.

7

Movement for psychologically disturbed children

This chapter describes activities which can help those children with whom it is difficult to make relationships. These are children who actively avoid relationships; they present us with a particular challenge. They are rewarding to work with but they may be very testing. Such children have individual needs and the following examples are included here to show how relationships can be developed in different ways.

Children with autistic tendencies

These children can be helped to relate on a one-to-one basis.

Stephen was tall for his age, pale with delicate features, and joined in movement sessions in his school for children with severe learning difficulties with the help of an older boy from a school for children with moderate learning difficulties. Stephen had movement sessions over a period of three or four years. During this time he acquired the confidence to join in all the activities and voluntarily committed himself to being supported by older children. He made progress through participating in simple and non-threatening partner experiences (as described in Chapter 1). He slowly learnt both to trust other people and to trust himself.

One young woman in an adult training centre initially resisted partner work. She gradually gained confidence and began to relate to a partner, losing her strong resistance to physical involvement. Over the space of a year she began to enjoy relationship play partly through seeing the enjoyment and participation of the others in her group.

A postgraduate student spent one day a week for six weeks trying to make a study of a small boy with autistic tendencies. Like so many similar children, he loved music and watching the record player. He avoided contact with the other children and was always on the edge of the classroom. He consistently avoided the student by running away from her. Towards the end of her study, I was asked to supervise her, and I suggested that we went into the school hall. There I slid the boy along the floor by his ankles so that he could enjoy the free flow of sliding. I obtained good eye contact with him because he was surprised to see someone so much higher than he was in this unfamiliar situation. I got down to floor level and worked with him carefully, doing see-saws and cradling, then asked the student to place the boy astride my back while I was on all fours. In this position I swayed gently forwards and backwards, and when I felt he was secure, I took him for a careful ride. At the end of about ten minutes of playing together, I sat down with the boy between my legs and he leant back against me. He was relaxed, trusting me. I then asked the student to go through the series of activities which I had just done with the boy, which she did. When the student and boy stood up to leave the hall, the boy lifted up his arms, indicating silently that he wanted her to pick him up. The student was very moved because, after weeks of frustration, she had at last got through to him.

Hyperactive children

There are various strategies which can be used to relate to hyperactive children.

On one occasion a physiotherapist lay across and on top of a particularly noisy and energetic boy in a hospital in Norway. She squashed him, and used her body to roll him. This had an immediate effect and from then on he related to her, and he no longer ran shouting round the hall. In the same session another boy who could not speak but could only grunt, lay on the floor on his back shaking an arm and a leg in the air, demanding to be swung. He got his swing but he was swung round with his back sweeping the floor by a student, so that he had the free-flow experience combined with being earthed at the same time.

I was once in a school hall with a highly disturbed group of children. One boy ran constantly round the hall. I caught him in mid-flight, held him round his waist facing away from me, gave him a swing and then released him. He continued running. I caught him and swung him again. I did this three or four times. Then my attention was distracted and I failed to catch him. I felt a tap on my shoulder and there he was asking for a swing. The fact that I had to hug him tightly went unnoticed because the free-flow swing was so enjoyable.

On only two occasions have I had to ask teachers to hold onto their child partners and not to let them go because the children's main aim was to run away and be chased. The first time I assigned one hyperactive boy in a mainstream school 'nurture class' to an experienced movement teacher because I knew that she would be able to cope with him. He succeeded in escaping once and I caught him and returned him to his partner. The teacher made relationship play such fun and so rewarding that the boy no longer wanted to run away and found it was more enjoyable to stay with the teacher.

On the second occasion a very active boy of eight was partnered by a woman teacher who could not cope with him. I asked her to make a 'house' with her body and hold the child firmly inside and let him watch the session. He watched the movement activities of his class and when the session was over and the other children had left, this boy went into the middle of the hall and proceeded to do, by himself, the activities which he had been watching. This took place at a teacher's centre in Brisbane and some of the teachers in the morning group returned in the afternoon to see what the boy would do in the second lesson that day. When the boy returned in the afternoon he joined in quite normally with the other children, to everyone's surprise.

An extremely hyperactive boy came with a group of children with severe learning difficulties to work in the college gymnasium once a week for eight weeks. We made no progress with this boy. He flitted from one piece of apparatus to another. His favourite place was in the dark apparatus cupboard where he sang to himself. He would not speak but his choice of song often expressed what he was feeling. The boy's partner was a man with children of his own but he found it difficult to relate to the boy. On the last session the boy worked with a woman student on a crash mat. She was able to communicate through physical play, and the boy felt happy with her. He climbed over and under her, rolled and somersaulted, and stayed with her for the longest period he had stayed anywhere pursuing one kind of activity. At the end of the session the boy's male partner made a 'house' on all fours and the boy crept inside and stayed there. We were sad that this was our last session with the group, as we could not build on the progress that had been made. The boy's parents said the only nights their son slept well were after the days he came to our gymnasium. As he grew older the boy became more uncontrollable and his parents had to place him in a subnormality hospital.

Children who avoid relationships

While working with teenagers with severe learning difficulties in Toronto, I was told that one girl would not let anyone touch her. This is not unusual, but it is possible to help a child eventually to forget to avoid contact and to join in the activities which the rest of the children are enjoying. In this case the girl saw how much the other teenagers in her class were enjoying lying on the backs of others and being swayed gently, and she could not resist climbing onto the backs of three people side by side on all fours (see Fig. 16). She lay on them face down and they swayed her gently. Teaching staff who knew her well were most surprised.

Another teenage girl with severe learning difficulties would not let anyone near her; her reaction was to swear and to spit. However, she wanted to bounce on a trampette and accepted the support of two students – one on each side of her and therefore not face to face, which might have been more threatening. She also allowed someone to push her on a swing, another free-flow experience. She had an excellent class teacher and learnt to do forward somersaults over the teacher's shoulder. Initially she refused, saying, 'I will hurt you. I am too heavy for you,' but gradually she copied others in the class and became adept at somersaults (see Fig. 17). She was not threatened by being supported and enfolded by the teacher. She went on to an adult training centre where she joined in all the movement and physical education activities going on there.

Children learn a great deal from watching each other, so it is helpful if children who resist involvement with others are in a class with children who are not inhibited in the same way. A mixed-ability group of children can lead to a richer movement experience for all.

Maria was about twenty-two. She lived in a hostel but before that had spent many years on a ward in a subnormality hospital. She twiddled a shoelace all day and was isolated; when approached she could be extremely violent. I worked with her for just one hour on a teachers' course, but I felt I had to take a risk and invade her isolation.

A group of five teachers and physiotherapy students were working with her and observing her. We started by trying to give her a swing, holding her round the waist; this she violently resisted. Then we tried to swing her with four people holding her limbs; this she accepted only reluctantly. The only activity she allowed was to be slid along the floor, which was a step forward. A great deal was going on in the gym and she could see other people from her hostel enjoying themselves. She eventually allowed herself to be played with and cradled by a student physiotherapist who showed great maturity and courage because Maria had already attacked another student. The student cradled Maria and stroked her arms; when she stopped, Maria indicated by taking the student's hands that she wanted this to be continued. They had face-to-face eye contact and a lot of fun together. Maria seemed to know that this particular person was not afraid of her. At the end of the session the student and Maria sat hand in hand, talking, waiting for the bus to take Maria back to the hostel. It was hard to believe it was the same girl.

Unfortunately the staff in the hostel could not give Maria the attention she needed because of the demands of the hostel's many other residents who were more amenable and less violent. However, relationship play was subsequently implemented for the other residents in the hostel.

Disturbed people, children and adults, know at once if others are afraid of their reactions; they also know that fun, humour and play have a great contribution to make towards diffusing anger and violence. Some of those who work with disturbed people have enormous resources, but this session with Maria stretched those of us who worked with her to our limits.

At one time I worked in a neuro-psychiatric clinic in Rome with very disturbed young children. One boy was totally isolated; he moved around shuffling on his bottom and was only interested in objects in a box. I lay on the ground beside him and looked up at him. He was not used to seeing people below him and he gave me the deep look I have occasionally had from very disturbed children. From then on he acknowledged my presence. Speech therapy students partnered these isolated and disturbed children with great sensitivity. On the second day I was asked to show how the children could work with each other. This was a tall order, but by the end of the session one child was able to cradle another, which was surprising, as the children had very little to give each other. The people watching were very moved to see that such disturbed children could be so gentle with each other.

Emotionally and behaviourally disturbed children

Children in schools for the emotionally and behaviourally disturbed are those who have suffered emotional damage and cannot be contained in a mainstream school. These children have a great need to experience security, both emotional and physical. The children find it very difficult to make relationships, either with adults or with other children.

Working with disturbed children is challenging, rewarding, and extremely interesting. As the children are afraid to commit themselves to a relationship, work with them depends very much on their relationship with a member of staff on whom they can rely.

All children love to play, so activities have to be presented in an unthreatening and enjoyable way. Figures 16, 17 and 27 are all photographs of emotionally and behaviourally disturbed boys, which were taken by their house parent. She started movement play with a small group of about six boys before bedtime. They got into their pyjamas and used a space which was carpeted and had easy chairs. The house parent slowly built up the boys' confidence in her, and then in each other, until they were prepared to support each other. Eventually, after experiencing different ways of supporting each other, one boy was able to cradle another. It is always difficult for emotionally damaged children to get close to their feelings, so it is an achievement when one boy can be gentle with another. The boys took part in the movement sessions as fun, and did not realise the philosophy underlying their activities.

Emotionally and behaviourally disturbed children are usually quite intelligent, if not very intelligent, and they can develop ideas quickly. They can also make dramatic progress when they find it is safe to trust another person. The quality of the member of staff, or of the partner, makes a marked difference to the child. It is noticeable that very disturbed children have the ability to see which partner will be able to help them, someone they can respect and trust. In the case of student teachers, such a child will often choose the psychologically mature student. The more disturbed the child is, the more he or she will test the partner.

Many emotionally and behaviourally disturbed children take refuge in a fantasy world, and dramatic play may be a natural progression from movement. Disturbed children in schools for children with severe learning difficulties respond to dramatic play, and it is clear that some of them lead a rich internal fantasy life.

When working with emotionally and behaviourally disturbed children, progress can be relatively quick, whereas when working with children with severe learning difficulties, progress is slow but usually steady and is therefore rewarding.

Elective mutes

Children who are elective mutes often respond well to movement and dramatic play. In one nurture group a boy said 'Bye bye' at the end of his third movement session, much to the delight of his teacher.

Teacher qualities

Ideally, the teacher or caregiver who works with psychologically disturbed children needs to have the following qualities.

1   *Emotional stability*
Emotional stability and physical stability develop together; sometimes they are acquired during childhood, sometimes they are learnt to some degree during training, and sometimes they are present in the adult as a result of life experiences. The emotionally mature person knows where he or she stands; what behaviour he or she can accept; and how to cope with unacceptable behaviour. Disturbed children may test adults to their limits so that the adult has great need of inner resources.

Some teenagers are more equipped to give stability to disturbed children than some adults.

2   *The capacity to relate to the disturbed child*
The adult has to find the strengths, the growing points, in each child. This may be the result of intelligent observation, or may be the result of a decision made intuitively though based on experience. The adult needs to give the child his or her value, respect the child, and build on what the child has to give. Encouragement, appreciation, firmness about boundaries of behaviour, and constant availability, are part of the treatment involved.

The adult has one foot in the child's world and one foot in the adult's world. People who are separate can make a relationship, so the adult who is sympathetic and understanding also needs to regard the child objectively. In many ways they relate as equals; the adult learns to relate to a child who has been emotionally damaged, and the child learns to trust the adult.

3   *A sense of humour and an ability to play*
When activities are presented in the form of enjoyable play, the disturbed child finds them less threatening. Disturbed children find it difficult to commit themselves to a relationship with another person or even to allow the proximity of other people. Some disturbed children find it very difficult to play but they are attracted towards play activities, and if they can trust the adult then progress can be made.

4   *Directness and honesty*
Disturbed children usually have insight and an intuitive perception about other people, so any pretence on the part of adults will be noticed. These children may reject contact with adults because the children do not pretend and are on the lookout for adult deceptions.

5   *Resilience and stamina*
Working with disturbed children is demanding and exhausting both emotionally and physically. Teachers and caregivers need to find ways of re-charging their batteries so that they do not become

depleted. Working as a member of a team who are all operating with the same values and ideas will help the individual.

Part Five

DEVELOPMENTAL MOVEMENT:
a summary

Developmental movement: a summary

Each teacher or caregiver can make use of the material described in this book in his or her own way. Teachers develop their own variations and ideas, as do the children they teach.

Movement sessions can provide a preparation for many other physical activities. Children benefit from a rich and comprehensive programme and ideally this should include work with apparatus, swimming, outdoor pursuits, sports of all kinds, and different types of dance and movement activities as preparation for drama. All these activities are tackled more confidently if children have developed some degree of body mastery and have learnt to adapt and relate to other people. Developmental movement can provide a basis from which children can explore other activities.

It will be noticed that there is no element of competition in the movement experiences described here; everyone is successful in some way and everyone is praised and encouraged to pursue further effort.

Teachers have used the developmental movement described here with partially sighted and blind children, and with physically handicapped children, with encouraging results. The development of body awareness and relationships to others are significant for both these groups. These methods have also been used with hearing impaired and profoundly deaf children, who have proved responsive and quick to learn.

Developmental movement can help children in two main areas:

1 *Physical development*
- Children experience what it means to feel 'at home' in their own bodies.
- They learn to use and control their bodies in many different ways and acquire a balanced movement vocabulary.
- Emphasis is not on acquiring particular skills for certain sports or activities, but on developing general skills in the mastery of many aspects of movement which can be applied to different physical tasks the children may meet.

2 *Development of personality*
- Children acquire a stronger sense of self, of their identity, through developmental movement.
- They become more confident in their own abilities.
- They learn to use their initiative and inventiveness.
- They learn to be sensitive to the needs and feelings of others and become more skilled in communicating and sharing experiences with other people.
- They learn to focus attention on what they are doing and to learn from movement experiences.
- Children experience a sense of achievement and fulfilment when developmental movement is well taught.

Summary of activities in Chapters 1 and 2

Activity	Page no.	Development of child
1 **Developing relationships**		
Caring or 'with' relationships		
Containing		
1 Cradling	5	security · relaxation · trust
2 Containing with support – 'rocking horses'	8	commitment of weight · sense of play
3 Containing with falling	8	security · sense of play
Supporting, commitment of weight		
4 Astride caregiver's stomach	10	trust · eye contact
5 Astride caregiver's back, caregiver lying down	10	trust · gripping with legs
6 Caregiver sitting, bouncing and patting child's back	11	awareness of stomach and back · comfort · rhythmical movement
7 Slide over caregiver's curled-up body	16	experience of body against caregiver
8 Caregiver sitting, child standing on thighs	16	balance · confidence · concentration
9 Caregiver on all fours ('horse'), child lying on caregiver's back	16	trust · relaxation
10 Caregiver on all fours, child astride back	16	gripping with arms and legs · commitment to relationship
11 Caregiver sitting, child standing on bent knees	16	balance · confidence · concentration
12 Caregiver on all fours, child on all fours on back	18	balance · confidence · concentration
13 Caregiver on all fours, child standing on back	18	balance · confidence · concentration
14 Three, four or five people on all fours, child lying on their backs	18	trust · relaxation
15 Aeroplanes	18	trust · confidence · eye contact
16 Somersaults	21	trust · awareness of centre of body · weight transference · body awareness against caregiver

Activity		Page no.	Development of child
	Rolling		
17	Caregiver sitting, rolling child up and down body	11	awareness of the body against caregiver · flexibility in trunk
18	Double roll	11	being contained and squashed (gently!) · awareness of body against caregiver
19	Child rolls caregiver	11	initiative · concern for partner · responsibility
20	Horizontal rocking	11	relaxation · awareness of body against mat or floor
	Sliding		
21	Sliding	13	relaxation · flexibility in spine · eye contact
	Tunnels		
22	Caregiver on all fours	13	initiative · exploration
23	Several caregivers' tunnels	13	initiative · exploration
24	Long line on all fours · child creeping underneath · child creeping along top	13	confidence · exploration awareness of body against backs · concepts of 'under', 'through', 'over', 'on top'
	Gripping		
25	Caregiver lying on stomach, child astride back	16	gripping with legs · commitment of weight
26	Caregiver on all fours	16	gripping with arms and legs · commitment to relationship
27	'Baby monkeys'	18	strength · commitment to relationship
28	Mutual hug, caregiver standing	21	confidence · shared commitment · strength

Activity		Page no.	Development of child
Parts of the body			
Awareness of knees			
2	Non-weight bearing	42	sensory input of knees · inventiveness
3	Weight-bearing, kneeling	42	sensory input of knees · inventiveness
4	'Open/shutting animal'	43	awareness of centre, elbows and knees
5	'Little legs'	43	discovery of different forms of locomotion and directions in space
6	Standing, knees bent	43	locomotion · directions in space · inventiveness · mobility in hip joint
7	'High knees'	43	elevation flight and free flow · mobility in hip joint
8	Skipping, galloping	44	control of knees · elevation
9	'Funny walks'	44	inventiveness · humour
Awareness of hips			
10	Spinning	46	hips felt against floor · free flow
11	Somersaults	46	experience of high hips and hips against floor
12	Balancing in twos	46	control of hips under body and over feet
Awareness of trunk and centre			
13	Rolling	47	trunk felt against floor · free flow · flexibility in spine
14	Sliding	47	back felt against floor · flexibility in spine · free flow · relaxation
15	Creeping	47	front of body felt against floor · flexibility in spine · coordination of limbs
16	'Parcels'	48	experience of a 'home' · body is close to itself · strength
17	Somersaults	21, 48	maintaining centre · transference of weight
18	Twisting roll	50	flexibility in trunk · free flow
19	Rolling in ball shape	50	transference of weight · free flow
20	Falling		
	· from lying	10, 50	relaxation · free flow
	· from all fours	52	transference of weight · free flow
	· from standing	52	management of body weight · free flow ·
	· from jumping	52	transference of body weight

Children's comments

The following are extracts from comments written by 12-year-old children from a middle school about their movement classes with young children with severe learning difficulties.

We do things like give them bumpy rides, make tunnels, stick them to the floor and try to push them over etc. The little girl we (my partner and me) had was called Andrea, and she was so cheerful. It was nice to see her enjoying it, but inside she could be hurting. So we try to relive the pain by being happy ourselves and by doing activities with her and it worked. People think that they're just an empty sole, but there not they feel, see, smell, touch, love, hate, hurt and be happy. so they're just the same as us, but they can't use them the way we do. I found their strengh hard because they're so strong. I think they find mixing with people hard because people don't want to know them, and I don't like that at all.

Rebecca

I worked with a girl called Helen who had difficulties with the things we take for granted like walking, sitting and just staying still. It was nice to do things with handicap children because when you saw them enjoying themselves It made you feel proud because you had helped this child to do what it can.

clare.

I feel that handicapped children need to work with normal children and like working with normal children. The handicapped children do things they wouldn't normally do and learn different things. I like working with them because they are nice to talk to and its nice to see handicapped children enjoying themselves. I think there are quite a few things that Whittlesea children find hard but they try their best even though they have disabilities.

Joanne

The first time we had P.E. with the handicap children I was amazed in the way that you make friends straight away and I was surprised at the helpers who just treated the handicap children like there was nothing wrong with them one of the helpers said to me "be firm with him hes being rather naughty today" I could'nt see what was wrong with his behavier he seemed well behaved enough to me. We don't get much time with them but the time we do get is a lot of fun

Paul

P.E with the Whittlesea children was a lot different to a normal P.E lesson. Because in a usual lesson we dont have to work as hard were being taught, but with the Whittlesea kids we were teaching them. we done all different activities like bumpy rides, briges, trying to push each other over when we were in a strong position, and we done a lot more. I think that sherborne P.E. is very good for the children. it's not only good for the whittlesea kids. Its also good for us.

David

The difference between P.E with Whittlesea and a usual P.E lesson is you have to be a lot more patient with Whittlesea because they don't understand things as well as we do. We done a lot of activities with the little children and it was fun for both them and us. The Whittlesea children are no different to us except their ability to do things and the way they were born, its not their fault they have turned out like that. The thing i enjoyed the most was back to back.

viren

When we do P.E. with the handicapped children the things we do are a lot different from normal P.E. lessons, and I found it alot easier and I am not really very good at P.E. but the teachers explained that it helps them and mostly thier stomach muscles. Sometimes the boy or girl may find it a bit difficult to understand you so you learn a few simple hand sighns like stand, sit and lie down. Sometimes when the boy or girl is supposed to lie down and relax, as you straighten them out you notice just how tense their muscles are because they are not aware that they have muscles in those places.

Daniel.

Useful resources

Books

BIMH = British Institute of Mental Handicap, Wolverhampton Road, Kidderminster

Bettelheim, B. *A good Enough Parent* Chapter 13 (Thames and Hudson, 1987)

Finnie, N. *Handling the Young Cerebral Palsied Child at Home* 2nd edn (Heinemann, 1974)

Groves, L. *Physical Education for Special Needs* (Cambridge University Press, 1979)

Hollis, K. Progress to Standing (BIMH, 1977)
Progress to Improved Movement (BIMH, 1983)

Jennings, S. (ed.) *Creative Therapy* Chapter 3 'Creative play with babies' (Kemble Press, 1983)

Laban, R. *Modern Educational Dance* 3rd edn (Northcote House Publishers, 1988) *Mastery of Movement* 4th edn (Northcote House Publishers, 1980)

Leboyer, F. *Loving Hands. The traditional art of baby massage* (Collins, 1977)

Liedloff, J. *The Continuum Concept* Chapter 3 'The beginning of life' (Penguin, 1986)

Reid, M. *Handling the Disabled Child in Water* (Physiotherapy Dept, Brays School, Brays Road, Birmingham B26 1NS, 1976)

The Sports Council Pamphlets   *2 Lifting and Handling; 3 Swimming and Epilepsy; 5 Medical Considerations* (The Co-ordinating Committee on Swimming for the Disabled, the Sports Council, 16 Upper Woburn Place, London WC1H 0QP)

Thornton, S. *A Movement Perspective of Rudolf Laban* (Macdonald and Evans, 1971)

Upton, G. *Physical and Creative Activities for the Mentally Handicapped* Chapters 1, 2, 3 (Cambridge University Press, 1979)

Whiting, H. *Personality and Performance in Physical Education and Sport* Chapter 'The body concept' (Henry Kimpton Publishers, 1973)

York-Moore, R. *Management of the Physically Handicapped Child* Pamphlet No. 1, 2nd imprint (BIMH, 1983)

Films and videos

In Touch   Movement for mentally handicapped children   1965
Explorations   Movement for drama   1971
A Sense of Movement   Movement for mentally handicapped
                                                children   1976
A Matter of Confidence   Movement for children and parents in a
                                                socially deprived area   1980
Building Bridges   Movement for mentally handicapped adults   1982
Good Companions   Movement for normal and handicapped
                                                children (video)   1986

Distributed by Concord Films Council, 201 Felixstowe Road, Ipswich, Suffolk

*Selected for preservation by the National Film Archive